Arabische Welt - Arab World

Band 3

Arabische Welt - Arab World

Band 3

Herausgegeben von Rüdiger Lohlker

Alisa Douer

The Israeli-Palestinian Conflict

Guilt on Both Sides

Logos Verlag Berlin

λογος

Bibliografische Information der Deutschen Nationalbibliothek

Die Deutsche Nationalbibliothek verzeichnet diese Publikation in der Deutschen Nationalbibliografie; detaillierte bibliografische Daten sind im Internet über http://dnb.d-nb.de abrufbar.

Photographs: Archive Moshe Douer

Coverfoto: Moshe Douer on the right side in British army uniform With a Palestinian counterpart, around 1948

ISBN 978-3-8325-4129-3
ISSN 2199-4013

Logos Verlag Berlin GmbH
Comeniushof, Gubener Str. 47,
10243 Berlin
Tel.: +49 (0)30 / 42 85 10 90
Fax: +49 (0)30 / 42 85 10 92
http://www.logos-verlag.de

Dedicated to my Sephardic father
Moshe Douer
Who, through his attitude and actions,
taught me to appreciate my fellow humans

Meeting on the opening day of the road to Teybe (an Arabic village) about 1950
Moshe Douer is the second from left in British army uniform

Personal Note

For a dream of peace we should never abandon.

To begin, I would like to recount my childhood in Tel Aviv and Jaffa.

I was born in Palestine, a region under British Mandate from 1923 to 1948. Nevertheless, I was always an Israeli, with a Yiddish-speaking grandmother on one side and Arabic-speaking grandparents on the other.

My mother's family emigrated from Lithuania to Palestine in 1931. My father's family came from Halab (Aleppo), Syria, at the end of the 19th century—where they lived ever since they had to leave Spain in the late 1500s.

My father was a governor on behalf of the British Mandate. He was in charge of three Arab villages in Wadi-A'rra, a region between Tel Aviv and Haifa. (These villages still exist.) As a child, I would often accompany him on his visits. While the adults were talking and eating, we children used to play, ride on donkeys and eat fruits directly from the trees of the *bustan*—as orchards are called in Arabic. It did not occur to me that Arab children were different from me; it was just fun to be in the villages and play together.

My grandfather owned a leather workshop in Jaffa, a city that both Arabs and Jews called home. As children, we used to play in the streets, and we called all the adults uncles and aunts. Being Arab or Jewish was not an issue for any of us.

All this changed in May 1948, when the state of Israel was founded. I cannot pinpoint a certain day when this change occurred. I was yet a small child, but all of a sudden my father stopped going to the villages and I no longer visited my grandfather's shop in Jaffa. The carefree relations between Arabs and Jews ceased to exist; I could not understand why we were now supposed to hate "them" or how "they" had become our enemies. Nobody in my family had ever told me that Arabs were bad people. To this day, I cannot comprehend such feelings of hatred: this is largely due to my education and especially to my father.

A Note of Thanks

First of all, I would like to remember in gratitude my father, who taught me tolerance and who continued to have many Arab friends, even after 1948.

I am particularly grateful to Professor Rüdiger Lohlker, who encouraged me to write this book.

I thank to all the people who have written about the Middle East and the Israeli-Palestinian conflict, thereby affording me a good overview of the subject.

I would also like to thank my friends: Barbara Hulan, Vera Kofler-Mongold, Peter Röhsler, Nicholas Steinhoff, who patiently listened to me when I was writing this book and provided thoughtful comments on the topic.

Special thanks go to the Israeli newspaper *Haaretz* and its journalists for their contributions and open-mindedness about the Palestinian question—a unique attitude in the Middle East.

I would like to express my gratitude to my son Nitsan Bazelet, who read and made important comments on the book, and to Karin Hanta-Davis for style-editing the manuscript and raising many questions in the process.

Table of contents

Introduction

We should not argue who is to blame (Israel or Palestine)
There is enough guilt on both sides. / Uri Avneri

You realize your ties to a country are strong when its policies annoy and anger you, and you feel helpless because you are not able to change them.

The Israeli-Palestinian conflict is a never-ending story. It has been going on *de jure* since the declaration of the state of Israel on May 15, 1948. *De facto* it started much earlier, in 1920, with the beginning of Arab revolts against the British occupation/Palestinian Mandate, which increased in intensity as time went by and reached its climax in the Arab Revolt from 1936 to 1939.

Political problems have been a part of everyday life in the Middle East, but with the influx of Jews into Palestine in the early 20th century, the conflict became acute for Arabs who had been living there for hundreds of years. They saw their land taken by the newcomers. They saw the desert transformed into a fruitful country, and came to realize that if this process continued, this place would no longer be their home. Which is precisely what happened.

Jews found it increasingly difficult to lead a normal life in Europe in the late 19th and early 20th century: in Russia and Poland, pogroms against them lasted from 1881 to 1919. Antisemitism also took on aggressive dimensions in Western Europe, reaching its climax in World War II (1939-1945) and the Holocaust, in which six million Jews were killed and hundreds of thousands displaced.

When the United Nations General Assembly discussed the partition of Palestine into two countries — Israel for the Jews and Palestine for the Arabs — in 1947, Europe breathed a sigh of relief: this plan looked like the perfect solution for displaced Jews who were neither keen on returning to their native countries nor readily welcomed by most of Europe. There were many reasons for this:

People in European countries were not able to look their victims in the eyes.

The perpetrators were not willing to give survivors back what they had stolen from them.

Europe was poor and ravaged by the war.

European governments would have had to find jobs and housing for Jewish survivors.

Most Jewish survivors were afraid of a new wave of antisemitism.

Therefore, a partition seemed like the best solution to everybody — except to the Arabs. It meant that the Jews were removed from Europe, out of sight of their torturers, who could forget, or at least suppress their guilty conscience towards the victims.

In the end, the Jews and the Palestinian Arabs had to pay the bill: Palestine was not the first choice of country for most Jews to settle in. However, given that they were not readily received in other European countries, many Jews went to Palestine. In this process, a large part of the landed property of the Arabs was taken away through legal means — such as land purchases by the Jews — or illegally when Arab land defined as '*rehush natush,*' abandoned property, was confiscated.

It was these land deals that triggered the Arab-Israeli conflict. For many reasons — as this book closely examines — this conflict remains unresolved.

In general, we can say that, after sixty-five years of war, terror and bloodshed, every reasonable person must be interested in bringing an end to the conflict. The time has come for the voice of reason to resound loudly and clearly, calling for the creation of a "normal" status quo in which both groups live together, side by side, in peace.

Many questions are left to be asked, and we can offer satisfactory answers to only a few of them. Leaders on both sides are either unwilling to talk to each other or lack the skills to do so. At times it seems almost as if they do not consider peace a serious issue. It seems almost as if leaders on both sides keep making one mistake after another because they do not want or are afraid to make decisions. In spite of the many factions on both sides -- religious groups, right-wing fanatics, and people in favor of a one-state solution (an impossible illusion, because in the end, both peoples will each have a part of former Palestine), both countries will continue to exist.

No matter who is right or wrong, history has brought two ethnicities to live together in this certain region. They have no other choice than to get along with each other.

'National consciousness' in the region developed because of historical events which were neither in the hands of the Jews nor of the Palestinian-Muslims. This 'invented reality' lets us understand the behavior of both peoples, but it does not provide us with the tools to reconstruct history. There is always a gap between what Israelis and Palestinians want and what they are able to achieve.

Why do Israelis and Palestinians hate and fear each other?

How did this situation get to a point where peace looks like an almost unattainable goal?

One of the purposes of this book is to analyze the central events in Israeli-Palestinian history in an effort to understand how and why the conflict can and must be solved — the faster the better.

In Jewish life, the wish to return to Zion was expressed in prayers and in Messianic movements. Modern Zionism, by contrast, was a secular movement dating to its inception in the 19th century. Its focus on Eretz Israel as the future homeland for the Jews was politically motivated. Zionism as a movement started to spread because of antisemitism in Russia and Poland (and later on, all across Europe). It was furthermore also related to the general emergence of national movements in Europe. "The Zionist intention was to build a new society based on the universal values of freedom, democracy, and social justice for all its citizens, without difference in religion, race, or gender. This society would be ruled according to the United Nations Human Rights Convention."[1] Unfortunately, some of these values were lost along the way — not only for Arabs, but also for other minorities (such as Jews from the Arab world who have faced discrimination in Israel.)

Since the first Zionist Congress in 1897, Zionist leaders have routinely ignored the Arab population of Palestine. Theodor Herzl (1860—1904), founder of political Zionism, spoke of a land that was supposedly uninhabited. He based his famous slogan, "A land without people for a people without a land," on this claim. In his programmatic book *The Jewish State* from 1896, he wrote that the only solution for antisemitism was for the Jews to have a state of their own. His book provided an organizational platform for political Zionism and laid the cornerstone for an international Zionist movement.[2] Nevertheless, it was not until antisemitism took violent turns in Germany starting in 1933, and later all over Europe, that European Jews started to seriously consider Zionist ideas. Until May 1948, hardly any Jews from Arab countries went to Palestine because there was no need for them to leave.

The concept of Eretz-Israel/Palestine refers to the 28,000-square kilometer territories between the Jordan River to the East and the Mediterranean Sea to the West. When I use one term or the other, I don't intend to transmit who has the rights to this territory.

The meaning of the term "settlement" includes the Jewish settlements that were established after the Six-Day-War in the the West Bank (1967 until today).

With the creation of the state of Israel in 1948, Palestinians faced the same destiny as Jews in Arab countries. About one million Jews had to flee or were expelled from across the

Arab world, forced in the process to leave all their possessions and properties behind. As they could not return to their home-countries even if they would have desired to, they suffered the same fate as Palestinian refugees.

A staggering amount of time and paper has been devoted to the Israel/Palestine conflict. I have studied many publications on the subject in a number of archives. Most are either pro-Israel and anti-Palestinian or anti-Israel and pro-Palestinian. This book seeks a third way.

The Jewish dream of regaining a homeland promised by God and the Arab dream of having a right to a land owned for centuries are no longer realistic.

Neither Jews nor Arabs will relinquish their claims to the land. A peaceful two-state solution is the only option.

Geography

Located between Egypt, Syria, Lebanon and Arabia, the Middle East is a region of foremost geopolitical interest. It is the birthplace of Judaism and Christianity and has had a long and tumultuous cultural and economic history. From the very beginning, the Israeli-Palestinian conflict was not only a political and regional one, but also a fight between cultures and religions for hegemony and control.[3] Since the Muslims invaded what we now call the Middle East in about 642 AD, the region has been controlled by numerous powers: until 1917 by Islamic rulers and from 1917 to 1948 by the British Mandate. After the Mandate came to an end, the state of Israel was founded.

Today the region includes Syria, Lebanon, Jordan, the West Bank, the Gaza Strip, and Israel. Before these states and territories came into being, Europeans called the region 'Syria' or 'the Levant.'[4] The region is also part of the "Fertile Crescent," which includes Egypt, Syria, Lebanon, Jordan, Mesopotamia (Iraq and parts of Persia), Palestine, and Israel.

Palestine is:[5]

"[A] [g]eographic name of rather loose application. Etymological strictness would require it to denote exclusively the narrow strip of coastal land. It is conventionally used as a name for the territory, which in the Old Testament is claimed as the inheritance of the pre-exilic Hebrews; except in the west, where the country is bordered by the Mediterranean Sea, the limit of this territory cannot be laid down on the map as a definite line. The Hebrews have preserved, in the proverbial expression 'from Dan to Beersheba' (Judg. xx, i & c - the northern and southern limits of their land), Eastward there is no such definite border but the river Jordan, which seems to be a natural border." Encyclopedia Britannica.

Origins

"The Arabs are Semites and belong to the same great racial group as the ancient Babylonians, Assyrians, Arameans, Phoenicians, and Hebrews. Being of kin, they must at some time have had a common original habitat. This common home of all Semites seems, according to scholars, to have been the Arabian Peninsula," writes Foster.

"The intimacy between Jews and Arabs is attested by the similarity of their language, by the Jewish historian Josephus, and by Muslim historians ... [and by] how ... Judaism held sway in South Arabia and by how, when Islam commenced, it had to deal with Jewish communities settled in the cradle of the system, the Hijaz," writes Foster.[6]

The Jewish dream of regaining a homeland promised by God and the Arab dream of having a right to a land owned for centuries are no longer realistic. Neither Jews nor Arabs will relinquish their claims to the land. A peaceful two-state solution is the only option.

As the Middle East is located close to the former Soviet Union, it became a central arena for Soviet-American competition long before the Cold War began. Wealthy Arab nations and Iran also started to engage in the fight for dominance in the region; this is why Arab as well as Israeli governments in the region have sought and received international support in their fight for existence. Many foreign governments have interfered in the region, either to reap economic benefits or attain hegemony. Few of them did so out of a real commitment to Israel or to the Arab countries. Establishing lasting peace in the region has never been a priority in world politics. Neither have the countries in the region themselves tried to reach a lasting peace accord. After World War II, the Cold War was one of the reasons for ongoing international involvement in the region, and therefore there was never any political stability in the region. After all, a lasting peace would have meant less foreign influence, which no foreign country was interested in.

Historically speaking, since the middle of the 17th century, Eretz Israel was part of (Greater) Syria and belonged to the Damascus province, as Wala'at-governed area. This province was divided into several sub-provinces: the Sanjaks (regions of Gaza), Jerusalem, Nablus, Lagoon, and Safed.[7]

In 1831, the Egyptian army under the command of Ibrahim Pasha,[8] started its march towards the North and invaded Palestine. It soon reached the city of Acre and conquered it from the Syrians and the Ottomans by holding a siege. Acre became Egypt's new power center on the Mediterranean Sea. The Egyptian rulers built new infrastructure such as markets, a port, and an aqueduct;[9] Acre remained under Egyptian rule until 1841, when it was retaken by the Ottomans.[10] Until the British army conquered the region in 1917, it remained under Ottoman rule.

Etymology

The name Israel first appeared on a stele in the grave of the Egyptian pharaoh Merneptah in 1209 BCE. The term Peleset—the root of the word "Palestine"—can be found in numerous Egyptian documents starting in 1150 BCE. It refers to a people or land neighboring Egypt.[11] As of circa 800 BCE, the Assyrians called the same region Palashtu or Pilistu. Neither Egyptian nor Assyrian sources establish clear regional boundaries for the land. The Hebrew name Pleshet is used in the Bible more than 250 times; the name is derived from the Plishtim, a people that lived in the region. It was never proven that the Palestinians of today are descendants of this people. This name continued to be used after the original people stopped being mentioned.

The region is also known by some other names that have been used to refer to all or some parts of the land: Canaan, Greater Israel, Greater Syria, the Holy Land, Judaea Province, Judea, Israel, Israel Ha'shlema—all of Israel, Kingdom of Israel, Kingdom of Jerusalem, Kingdom of Judea, Land of Israel, Zion, Eretz ha-zvi, Southern Syria, and Syria-Palestine. Most of the names listed above are used in the Old Testament—the Jewish Bible.

The boundaries of the region have changed throughout history and were last defined in modern times by the Franco-British agreement of 1920 and the Transjordan Memorandum of 1922, as the West Bank was put under Jordanian rule by the British in 1922-23, during the Mandate period in Palestine. Today the region includes the State of Israel, the West Bank, the Gaza Strip, and the Golan Heights, which are currently under Israeli occupation.

Exegesis

"I never doubted the right of the Israeli-Jews to live in a democratic, open and inclusive state of Israel which belongs to all its citizens. I never doubted the deep religious affinity of the Jews to their holy country. There is just no moral commitment between Israel and Palestine. ... Yet both radical Muslims and radical Jews doubt the right of Israel to exist. This is not only an anachronistic folly but also a recipe for further catastrophe in the region."[12] The Judea part of Israel became Palestine under the Romans in the second century CE. During this time, the name Eretz Israel also appeared for the first time,[13]

writes Professor Shlomo Sand in his two books, *How and When Was the Jewish Nation Invented* and *When and How Was the Land of Israel Invented.* Sand's views have sparked off controversy among many Israelis and among Jews around the world.
Palestinian intellectuals such as Muhammad Muzlah and Rashid Khalidi describe the state of Palestine as such: "Zionism motivated the Arabs of Palestine to organize themselves politically and to formulate their national ideology. The most important reason for this was a split in the Arab world, when Arab societies in different regions started to develop a national consciousness. Therefore, the obvious conclusion was that the Arabs of Palestine also created their own independent national movement."[14] Scholars such as the Palestinian intellectual Halil Sakhanini reject Zionism outright and express their hate of the state of Israel openly. He does not describe his national identity as Palestinian "because the entire land is Arabic."[15]

Historic Rights: Bible and Qur'an

Muslims ruled the region from 642 to 1917—first the Arab conquerors and then the Ottomans.[16] All in all, Palestine was under Muslim rule for almost 1,300 years.[17]
H.S. Karmi says that, as Jewish and Christian prophets are also holy to Muslims, it is logical that Jerusalem is holy to the three major monotheistic Religions. "Certain commentators ... put the three of them on an equal footing."[18]

The Bible

The Bible is not a historically reliable document. Nevertheless, it is taken seriously not only by Jews, but also by Christians and Muslims.
God promised the Land of Israel to the Hebrews—today called Jews—whose land extended from the Mediterranean Sea to the Jordan River 2000 years ago. According to Genesis, the first book of the Bible, God made this promise at least three times: to Abraham, to Isaac and to Jacob, the three founders of the Jewish faith.[19] In later books of

the Bible, this promise is mentioned repeatedly, attesting to the bond between God and the people of Israel.

The Qur'an

"Allah gave the earth to the Prophet, and it was bestowed upon him forever" (Qur'an 59: 6-7). The city of Jerusalem is holy to Muslims for several reasons: firstly, the story of the Prophet's Night Journey took place here in around 620 CE.[20] The Prophet also ascended to heaven from Jerusalem (Qur'an 17: 1). Twelve days after the death of the Prophet, the Muslim army invaded the region.[21] Secondly, Al-Masjid al-Aqsóa, the Dome of the Rock, the third holiest shrine in Islam after Mecca and Medina, is located in Jerusalem. This monument celebrated the arrival of a new faith in a city holy to Jews and Christians.[22]

Result

The fact that there are many holy Islamic monuments in Jerusalem does not mean that Muslims have the sole claim to it, as there are many Christian and Jewish monuments in Jerusalem as well. Muslims, therefore, don't have any more of a right to refer to Jerusalem as their capital than do Christians or Jews.

Ties to the Country

The idea that Arabs are bound to the soil on which they have lived for hundreds of years is valid. After the destruction of the Temple in 70 CE, most Jews lived outside the region. (It is a matter of intellectual debate whether this fact should be considered to have resulted in a diaspora.) It is also valid that Jews consider Palestine as the land of their forefathers and their native homeland, to which they can lay a rightful claim. For many centuries, Jews were not entitled to buy or own land in most European countries. As they were often driven out of various European countries, they were always on the move. Even when Jews considered themselves German or French, they were not bound to the soil of these countries. For the first time in Jewish history, Jews were entitled to own land—their own land—in Israel.

Over the course of time, Jews took up different non-agrarian occupations. They were merchants, craftsmen, and in the 19th century, became professionals such as doctors, writers, and architects.

Palestinians who have always lived on Palestinian soil also are entitled to remain there. This does not mean, however, that they have a right to the land of Israel. The entire situation is governed by an international customary right, which establishes that a people that has lived in a place for more than 30 years possesses a habitual right to stay there.

Eretz Israel

The bonds of the Jews to Eretz Israel cannot be ignored. These bonds did not just develop after World War II (although until the 1940s, very few Jews pursued the thousand-year dream of returning to their homeland.) It was not until 1933—when leaving Europe became a necessity and very few countries wanted to receive Jews—that Israel was no longer considered just a theoretical solution, but became instead a viable destination for emigration. Emigration to Israel was often closely linked to Zionist ideas. However, many Jews were drawn to the region less out of a Zionistic conviction than because the Nazis had taken over most of Europe.

One of the Zionist ideas about Israel was that the country was more or less uninhabited. That is how the slogan "a country without a people, for a people without a country" was coined. It was not until Theodor Herzl (1860-1904) visited Palestine that he became aware of the region's Arab population. The residents of Palestine were Arabs—not Palestinians in the view of the Zionists—and therefore they were able to stay in the country under Israeli rule, or move to any other Arab country.

Before the foundation of the state of Israel in 1948, there existed neither Palestinians nor Israelis, but Arabs and Jews who lived in Palestine side by side for hundreds of years without any major problems.

In its basic tenets, Zionism aimed at establishing a Jewish state—a homeland for the Jews in Eretz Israel—where Jews would not be subject to discrimination and persecution.

Characteristics of the Israeli-Jewish Society

"Israel considers itself, or at least is regarded, as an outpost of the West in the midst of a still hostile Eastern world. ... Israel thus has become a laboratory for the world. It has to do the job whether it likes it or not. The problem is that the East ... is mainly represented by Arabs, with whom Israel shares a long history. Two peoples have been in close contact with one another for thousands of years—sometimes as different nations, sometimes as different religions, sometimes even as different civilizations—and are now confronting each other in a totally new and very complex situation,"[23] notes S. D. Goitein.

For the first time in history, Arabs live in a Jewish state—and not Jews in an Arab state, as it was the case for thousands of years.

Modeling its society on a Western pattern, Israel has been confronted with a problem that "the world at large faces today: whether the culture of the West is strong enough to integrate the gigantic masses of Eastern people (in this case, Arabs) into one global civilization. The Arabs ... are still inclined to oppose the West and with it Israel as its closest representative."[24] The question therefore arises if integrating Arabs into Western societies should be a goal, or if understanding and respecting one another in matters of culture, history, tradition and religion could be enough. Goitein further states, "The state of Israel is an outpost of Europe transplanted to the Eastern (or Southern) shore of the Mediterranean. It can rely on the intellectual resources of the Jewish people at large."[25]

The strength of Israeli society is that it is a mixture of people from all over the world, who brought to the country their cultures, languages and traditions, even though Israeli society always modeled itself on Europe. Zionism has had at its core a Eurocentric attitude, which led to the discrimination of Jews from the Arab countries. Instead of including these Jews by making use of their expertise about Arab societies and cultures and their linguistic skills, the Israeli government ignored them. They were never asked to take part in Israeli-Arab peace talks.

The 19th Century

In the 19th century, writes Shamir, there was not an "Arabic nationality" in the common sense, and, "a cultural awakening happened prior to the national awakening. At the time of the Ottoman rule, the lines of nationality were extremely blurred. Identity was based on one's family, tribe and religious community, mostly Muslim (...) on one's pride in one's ancestors and on a deep relation to the Qu'ran and to the Arab language and culture as a miracle of accomplishment. An Arab national movement emerged at the end of the 19th century because a process of westernization had begun in the Middle East when Napoleon entered Egypt in 1808."[26]

Napoleon Bonaparte marched into the region with his army after he landed in Alexandria, Egypt, in 1808. Later he moved northward into Palestine, held Jaffa under siege and conquered it within four days. He then continued to the North and reached Haifa and Acre. Napoleon offered the entire population of the region—among them the Jews—the chance to gather under the French flag to "establish the old city of Jerusalem." Napoleon did not succeed, however, and soon had to leave the Middle East. According to Shamir, the appearance of Napoleon opened a window into Europe for the Arab world and caused the first of many culture shocks in the region.[27]

The fact that the Arab local society was backward in comparison to Europe came as a shock to the Islamic community. According to Shamir, Arab Islamic renewal movements were inspired by the ideal of the "Golden Age" of Islam.[28]

During World War I, Jamal Pasha, Ottoman governor of Palestine under the British Mandate, aimed primarily at eradicating Zionism. Pasha saw to it that more than 10,000 foreign-born Jews were expelled from the region and that Jewish institutions were disbanded. In 1917, all Jewish inhabitants of Jaffa and Tel Aviv were banished to the north of the country.[29] In the same year, the British army entered Jerusalem under General Edmund Allenby (1831-1936), and soon occupied all of Palestine. By that time, the Ottomans had staged a withdrawal. Although they had not yet relinquished their claim to the Middle East, they no longer had any decision-making power.[30]

The Middle East from 1918 onwards

"One fact that should not be forgotten is that not a single independent state—neither Arab nor Jewish—existed in the Middle East before World War I," writes Goitein. For hundreds of years, Muslims and Christian and Jewish minorities in Palestine were subjects of the respective rulers of the region. Whatever might be said about Arab nationalism, the fact remains that the present state of the Arab world was mainly created by external factors."[31] These factors include the end of the British Mandate—particularly in Palestine and generally in the Middle East—which went hand in hand with the UN-mandated Palestine partition of November 29, 1947 and with the foundation of the state of Israel on May 15, 1948.

In the secret Sixe-Pico Accord from May 1916, Britain and France divided the Middle East between them. Syria and Lebanon came under French rule, the rest under British—except for Palestine, which had a special status as a British Mandate territory.

In November 1917, the Balfour Declaration[32] was issued with the purpose of compensating for the injustice committed towards the Jews mostly in Europe by giving them a country of their own, a national homeland.[33]

Since the inception of the Mandate in Palestine, the British were aware of the animosity between Arabs and Jews. They set up numerous commissions and drafted many papers to study the problem. All of them came to the conclusion that the solution for the problems between Jews and Arabs would be a partition of the country between the two peoples. The question of how and when it should happen did not occur until 1947, when the British government decided to end the Mandate and to hand over responsibility for Palestine to the United Nations General Assembly.

Chaim Weizmann (1874-1952)[34]

Chaim Weizmann officially received the Balfour Declaration[35] from Lord Edmund de Rothschild, the representative of the Jewish people in England. The declaration was presented to Rothschild in 1917 by British Foreign Minister Arthur James Balfour. Weizmann was convinced of the Jews' moral superiority to the Arabs, a belief most Zionist leaders as well as non-Jewish Europeans also held and which was rooted in their Eurocentric arrogance.

As a result of the Balfour Declaration, a national Arab movement started to form under Haj Amin El-Husseini (1897-1974), the Grand Mufti of Jerusalem, who was one of the most important instigators of the Arab revolts in the years 1929 and from 1936 to 1939. In these revolts, the Muslim population of Palestine reached a reversal in the British approach to the Palestinian question, and brought the British to issue the White Book[36] of 1939, which reduced many of the privileges the Jews in Palestine were enjoying until that time.[37]

Jews took part in the British invasion of Palestine as well as in other stages of the war. The Zion Mule Corps[38] was established in about 1915 and fought on the British side. Around 1916, the second corps of Jewish volunteers, the "Jewish Legion," took over; it was comprised of 5,000 men and included founders of the future state of Israel such as Yitzhak Ben-Zvi (1884-1963)—later the first Israeli president—and David Ben-Gurion (1886-1973), later prime minister of Israel. After the Balfour declaration of 1917 was issued, many Jews reacted to the British call for support in the wartime effort by joining the British Foreign Legion. The Legion took part in the British invasion of Palestine. Jewish military units ceased their activities after World War I ended in 1918. Not one Arab soldier fought on the British side. Arabs were consumed with hatred towards British and French colonialists. As a result, they sympathized with the German and Italian regimes in both World Wars.[39]

Zeev Jabotinsky (1880-1940)

Zeev Jabotinsky, the founder of revisionist Zionism, wrote in one of his essays that the Arabs of Israel are not a mob but a living nation, and that they would never agree to any compromise as long as there was still hope that they could throw the Jews out of the region. Jabotinsky therefore called for an "iron wall" through which the Arabs could not break. "In the end, I hope and believe that both peoples will be able to live as neighbors in peace, but the only way is an iron wall, meaning a strong Israel." Jabotinsky thought that these two peoples could not live together because they had too many prejudices against each other and each one wanted the land for themselves. The wall was meant to be an interim solution, until the two peoples learned to accept each other.[40] Jabotinsky did not state when the wall should come down. According to him, it should remain as long as it was necessary. In the above-mentioned quote, Jabotinsky recognized the rights of the Arabs of Israel and their claim to nationhood. David Ben-Gurion[41] (1886-1973), one of the founders of the state of Israel, upheld another doctrine, which ran counter to Jabotinsky's. Ben-Gurion probably felt that he had to take an opposing view because Jabotinsky and he represented different ends of the political spectrum in Israel. He still implemented the Jabotinsky doctrine in his Arab policies, but for a long time the iron wall between Jews and Arabs was imaginary. Ben Gurion knew that the Arabs would under no circumstances accept a Jewish state in Israel unless they were forced to do so.[42]

The British Mandate in Palestine, 1918-1948

In 1918, Britain and France, the winners of World War I, agreed to divide the Arab region in the Middle East. This division was ratified by the League of Nations. Syria and Lebanon came under French rule, the rest of the territories under British occupation.[43] The system of mandates set up by the League of Nations (Article 22) was a compromise based especially on the Anglo-French declaration about the (former) Ottoman provinces of 1918.[44] Not all countries under British occupation became Mandate territories. Countries such as Egypt were simply under British colonial rule.

The British army invaded Palestine between 1917 and 1918, after having ruled Egypt since 1882; the British army marched from Egypt to the Northern part of Palestine. It kept moving towards Syria and forced the Ottomans out of the region. "The Balfour Declaration vaguely defined that the region was supposed to become a 'national home' for the Jews. Because of their Protestant and humanistic ideals, many members of the British cabinet were supportive of Zionism. Of course, imperialistic considerations also had to be taken into account. A Jewish state was also, in the opinion of the British, a sort of guarantee for a smooth operation of the Eastern part of the Suez-Canal."[45] The situation changed, however, when Arab revolts broke out in 1929 and a White Book was issued revising the rights of the Jewish population in Palestine as well as Jewish immigration quotas to the region.

On the basis of a League of Nations Mandate, the British started to administer Palestine after World War I. In 1920, the League of Nations' Interim Report on the Civil Administration of Palestine stated that there were 700,000 people living in Palestine, four-fifths of them Muslims. Some 77,000 were Christians, while the Jewish population numbered 76,000.

Arab Nationalism

"The fact is that there was little evidence of Arab nationalism before 1908 and none at all of a specific Arab-Palestinian variety. Before 1918, few if any of the Jewish settlers ever contemplated the possibility that Arabs and Jews might clash one day against each other in bloody battles,"[46] Moris notes. The notable families of Jerusalem included the Ha'tib Ha'ldi, Husseini, Nashashibi, Nasiba and Budeiri families. They had competed for prestige, wealth, social status, and political influence for hundreds of years. Palestinian society was characterized by a dual-feudal alignment between the Husseinis and their opposition. During the British Mandate, the Husseinis sold land to the Jews even if they officially condemned their arrival in the region.[47]

Nasser's claim that "Palestinian-Arabs owned Palestine" is simply not true—several wealthy Palestinian *efendis* owned large parts of Palestine. It is true that Palestinians had lived there for generations, and this is why they should have had a customary right to the land or parts thereof, even though for the most part they were vassals who worked on somebody else's land. Wealthy Arabs sold the land and could not care less about the peasants that leased it from them without any guarantees of rights. Jewish immigrants to Palestine were content to buy as much land as possible for the future state of Israel, sometimes for a price that was much higher than its market value. Still, Arabs keep blaming others—mainly Israel, the United States and Europe—for the present condition of Palestine. "The Arabs have a rightful claim to the land and the Zionists do not,"[48] writes Nasser. He does not give any explanations to prove his point. Many of the facts he writes about are correct, but his conclusions cannot always be accepted.

The original Palestinian Mandate included what today is known as Israel, the West Bank and Transjordan. The British entered into Palestine in 1917. They moved into the Jordan Valley and into northern Palestine in 1918; as a result, they occupied all of Palestine. The English name "Palestine" was officially revived by the British after the fall of the Ottoman Empire, and was applied to the part of the territory that was under British Mandate.

Rights to the Land

Archeological artifacts attest to the fact that Jews, Christians and Muslims have lived in the territory of Palestine for thousands of years.

Before Christianity started, Jews and pagans called this land their home. In about 636 CE, the region was invaded by Muslims. They forced the inhabitants to convert to Islam or to leave. These first Arab invaders ruled the Middle East until 1071 CE. Afterwards, it was controlled by numerous foreign rulers including the Ayyubids, the Mamluks,[49] the Ottomans starting in 1517,[50] and the British[51] from 1917 until 1948. The region was therefore under Muslim rule for about 1,300 years. For more than 800 years, it was under the rule of non-Arab, Islamic governments from outside the area.

The region named Palestine or Eretz Israel never had any definite borders and in the course of history often changed in size. The partition of the Middle East into countries and the creation of independent states took place from 1946 to 1948.

All this does not really matter for the solution of the Israeli-Palestinian conflict. The only thing that matters is that both peoples have the right to live in peace in close proximity to each other. As those are the conditions on the ground, it is up to these two peoples alone to find a solution. Both have the right to a life in peace; both do not have any other country to call their own. (And no country in the world wants to receive them anyhow.)

After the British Mandate

At the end of 1947, following World War II and the Holocaust, the British government terminated the Mandate and moved the responsibility for Palestine to the United Nations General Assembly, which soon adopted a resolution recommending a partition into an Arab state, a Jewish state, and a special international status for the City of Jerusalem. The Jewish leadership accepted the proposal, but the Arab Higher Committee rejected it. A civil war began immediately and ended with the Arab-Israeli War of 1948, after the declaration of the state of Israel.

Edward Said, one of the preeminent scholars on the Middle East in the United States, claimed that "the Palestinians that were driven out in 1948 after having lived in Palestine for hundreds of years, were unhappy victims of the movement whose whole aim had been to end the victimization of Jews by Christians in Europe." Hannah Arendt states, "The solution of the Jewish question merely produced a new category of refugees."[52] This is absolutely corrcct. It shows that European powers were interested in the creation of a Jewish state because they did not want to receive Jews back in their countries after World War II, and they were not willing to find a solution for Jewish refugees in Europe. In the end, writes Shlaim, the events of World War II and the Jewish tragedy of the Holocaust were the moral argument to create a Jewish state in Israel.[53]

Land of the Fathers

"The Israeli nation was designed in Eretz Israel, a country the Jews inhabited from at least 1200 BCE to 200 CE. When the Romans conquered the region in 63 BCE., they called this land Palestine in order to disconnect the Jews from the country to which they were bound,"[54] writes Moris.

A small number of Jews had been coming to Palestine for decades before the state of Israel was founded. It was not until 1933—when Hitler seized power first in Germany and after 1939 in most of Europe—that Jews started to actively flee from Europe, and Jewish mass emigration became a real threat to the Arab population of Palestine.

For most European Jews, Israel was not the first choice, even though the number of members of Zionist organizations in Europe had increased tremendously between the two World Wars. Until the Holocaust, Israel was merely a theoretical place of emigration—although Jews always mentioned Jerusalem in their prayers when they said, "Next year in Jerusalem."

Zionism

When political Zionism took shape at the end of the 19th century, Amos Elon describes it as follows: "Zionism was not yet challenged by Palestinian nationalists, Islamic fundamentalists or terrorists. Like other European movements of national liberation such as the Czech, the Irish, the Italian, and the Polish national movements, it was a child of the Enlightenment and the ideas of the French Revolution ... Among other things, it called for the separation of Church and State."[55] Theodor Herzl's idea was to create a 'new Jew', a free person not influenced by years of Diaspora and discrimination, who would live in an atheistic new Jewish state.

Zionism also served as a non-religious Jewish identity and a substitute religion. Before 1939, Jews had always yearned for Israel, but only in theory. This circumstance changed drastically, however, when the National Socialist regime came to power in Germany in 1933 and conquered most of Europe in the years to follow, all the while pushing to eliminate the Jews. Palestine had become a safe haven, and the utopian vision of the

Zionist movement had become a real opportunity for survival, as most countries did not accept European Jews. Developments in Europe were one of the reasons for the "Great Arab Revolt" against the British in Palestine, which started in April 1936 and lasted until 1939, aggravating the security of the entire region.[56]

Until the 1940s, the Zionist movement had neither the political nor the financial support of Jewish masses anywhere. If most Jews had been subscribing to Zionism, millions would have left Eastern Europe for the Holy Land rather than the United States, Western Europe or the Arab countries. "I think that Zionism has exhausted itself. Precisely because it accomplished its aims,"[57] yet "the Holocaust remains a basic trauma of Israeli society. It is impossible to exaggerate its effect on the process of nation-building,"[58] writes Amos Elon. Many scholars believe that Zionism has run its course and lost its relevance. Zionists realized their dream after World War II by creating the state of Israel. According to them, there is no one—except for about 24,000 Jews who have lived in the region for generations— who needs Zionism anymore. The Jews that live in Israel are Israelis; the ones who live elsewhere are Jews. Nobody needs to be a Zionist anymore. If Jewish people want to live in the country of their fathers, they can now do so. Jews living outside Israel cannot claim to be Zionist. They can be Jews, and they can support Israel—but they are no longer Zionists.

"Aliyah"[59] - Immigration (to Israel)

Aliyah is the word for the Jewish immigration movement to Palestine and later Israel. Except for about 24,000 Jews who had lived in the region for generations, most people made aliyah by coming to the Jewish settlements in Palestine and later Israel. The movement started in about 1882[60] with the group Hibat Zion, which was founded in Eastern Europe after the pogroms of 1881. Many Jews left for Palestine, some went to the United States and other countries. Until 1881, about 24,000 Jews and about 600,000 Muslims had lived in Palestine.

First Aliyah

The First Aliyah took place between 1882 and 1903. About two thirds of the Jewish population of 76,000 people had entered the country during the First Aliyah. Most of these people came to the region with the support of the Zionist movement because they had been persecuted in Russia and Poland. Zionism aimed at avoiding further persecutions and pogroms and at building a Jewish state as "a safe haven for the world's Jewry."

Most of the newcomers did not have any training in agriculture, which was necessary for the creation of new settlements and of a food-supply infrastructure for the cities. Baron Edmund de Rothschild (1916-2009) was the first to come to the newcomers' support. He set up wineries and built settlements such as Zichron Ya'akov and Rishon le'Zion.[61] In 1891, a new wave of persecutions and banishments of Jews from Russia set in, bringing several thousands of Jews to Palestine within a few months—even though the Turkish government allowed them neither to enter nor purchase land. The new immigrants circumvented these restrictions by bribing Turkish officials.

Second Aliyah

The Second Aliyah took place from 1905 to 1920, and included mostly Russian, Polish and Lithuanian Jews who left their places of origin after the Kishinev Pogrom and persecutions occurring from 1903 to 1905.[62] The Yishuv[63] in Palestine had also started to actively recruit people for aliyah because great numbers of farmhands were needed to cultivate the land in Palestine. In 1910, some 10,000 Dunam[64] in the Izreel Valley and other locations[65] were bought from the Sursuq, Suleyman, Nashashibi, Husseini, and Bay Naziff families.

After a number of Arab attacks on about 5,000 Jews had occurred in 1905 and Jews had bought more property in Jaffa, Tel Aviv was founded as a modern Jewish city on the Northern edge of Jaffa.[66]

In 1919, Haim Weizmann and Emir Feisal (1885-1933)[67] signed the following agreement, "The Jewish Agency will support the Arab demands in front of the Peace Commission, and in exchange, Emir Feisal will recognize the rights of the Jewish people to Palestine as their national home."[68]

Third Aliyah

The Third Aliyah took place from 1919 to 1923. The number of Olim[69] is estimated to have ranged from 35,000 to 37,500.[70]

They came in small groups, mostly from Eastern Europe and Russia. The funds for their passages as well as for the settlements and land acquisition was contributed by Baron Rothschild, Baron Maurice von Hirsch (1831-1896), and Jewish organizations outside of Palestine.[71] Until May of 1948, Jews continued to purchase land from landlords who mostly lived outside of Palestine in Syria or Lebanon, as well as from the Greek Patriarchate in Jerusalem. Jews were the only ones who were both capable of purchasing and interested in buying the land. Most of the Palestinian families abroad wanted to get rid of their territories, as they were often located in regions with harsh climates such as the Jordan Valley—in swamps and deserts. The new landholders had to take extensive and expensive measures to make the land fertile.[72]

The new country was to be an agricultural economy. New kinds of plants and fruits were grown, especially a wide variety of citrus fruits. Many new forests and groves were planted.

In 1922, shortly after the beginning of the British Mandate in Palestine, the Churchill government issued its first White Paper supporting the Balfour Declaration of 1917 to establish a "national home" for the Jews within the territory of Palestine as well as the rights of the Arab population to remain in the region.

Fourth Aliyah

The Fourth Aliyah took place from 1924 to 1929. This aliyah brought about 60,000 Jews to Palestine. It was the first aliyah that hardly included Halutzim[73] but consisted mostly of middle-class Jews, craftsmen, merchants, and industrialists. Jews had almost no other region in which to seek political asylum, not least because immigration quotas in the United States had fallen as a result of new laws.

About 80 percent of people coming in the Fourth Aliyah settled in cities such as Tel Aviv,[74] Haifa,[75] and in smaller numbers in Jerusalem. In 1928, during the Fourth Aliyah, religious Jewish groups from Eastern Europe immigrated to Palestine for the first time. The Jewish population in the region grew from 12 percent in 1922 to 19 percent in 1927.

The year 1929 started on a hopeful note, but ended with major riots and tumults by the Arab majority.

It was the first big Arab Revolt, with more to come. "One should not think that Jews and Arabs were friends, but they lived in relative peace side by side. The riots of 1929 started with an attack on the Jewish quarters of Jerusalem and a real massacre in Hebron."[76] The bloodshed continued all over the country with murder, destruction of property, and looting. About one hundred Jews died in these riots, about two hundred were wounded because the British army arrived too late to be of any help. Cities in which Jews and Arabs had coexisted for decades suffered the most. As a result, the British reversed all aliyah certificates and lowered immigration quotas of Jews in general.

In 1930, a second White Paper was issued. It reduced the quotas for aliyah to a minimum, and imposed further restrictions upon Jews. They were no longer allowed to buy land because it was determined that Arab farmers had to be protected. Jews might have brought agriculture and prosperity to the region,[77] but as most Arabs were Falahs,[78] they had to pay a high price by losing their jobs and their homes.[79]

1929 to 1939: Historical Background

When Hitler came to power in Germany in 1933, Jews became underdogs. Many of them saw the writing on the wall and started to leave Germany for other European countries, some of which subsequently came under Nazi occupation.[80] Abu-Lughhod's opinion is that "the British intention was to keep the colonization of Palestine going by giving the Jews a homeland." Professor Stevens of Lincoln University clearly illustrates in his essay "the dynamics of political interaction between Zionists and Great Britain within the framework of ... European expansion. ... With British military forces occupying Palestine, the Zionist succeeded in obtaining the long-awaited legitimization of their political colonization of Palestine."[81] As history has shown, the British could not cope with the Middle East, especially with Palestine, and shoved the responsibility onto the United Nations General Assembly. Abu-Lughhod gets the facts right, but analyzes them in too simplistic and subjective a way. The British had their interests in the Middle and the Far East, but as times changed and independence movements gained ground in other parts of the world, the British had to surrender most of their colonies in the 1940s, not only those in the Middle East. In addition, when the National Socialists gained dominance over almost the entire European continent, the Jewish search for a homeland became all the more urgent.

First Arab Revolt of 1929

Until 1929, the first years of the British Mandate in Palestine passed in relative tranquility, mainly because only a very small number of Jews came into the region[82]—because the British Mandate authorities had drastically reduced the garrison after the revolt of that year. The hatred of Arabs against Jews took violent turns in about 1929.[83] Jews were always favored by the colonial powers. With the emergence of nationalism in the Middle East, it became clear that colonialism was on the wane. As Jews were identified with European colonialism, Arabs started to attack the least powerful part of the chain—the Jews—who were an easier target than the British. Attacks on Jews supposedly also entailed fewer punitive measures.

In 1930, a new White Paper was issued by the British government, restricting Jewish immigration by reducing the number of immigration certificates necessary to enter the country. The White Paper of 1930 also reduced permissions for Jewish land purchases in Palestine.[84]

"Since 1929, when the fights between Arabs and Jews started in Palestine, there has been a competition between both sides about the question: who is the victim—the Arabs or the Jews? Each side remembers the acts of violence on the other side, emphasizes its victim status and points to the other side as the aggressor … this narrative has been part of each side's history since at least 1929, when bloody riots started under the British Mandate. ...

The mechanisms on both sides are identical. This is why nobody feels guilty about killing children and unarmed citizens,"[85] notes Hilel Cohen.

The non-Jewish population of the region—mostly Muslim Arabs—started to revolt against the British in 1920, to an increasing extent in 1929 and again from 1936 to 1939, because the British allowed Jewish immigration to Palestine, and again permitted Jews to purchase land.[86]

As the situation in Europe became increasingly dangerous for the Jews, many immigrated to Palestine, where the balance of power changed as tensions between Arabs and Jews escalated.

The British governed Palestine under the motto "divide et impera"[87] by stoking animosity between Jews and Arabs. Feelings of hatred against Jews flared up not only in Palestine, but also in Egypt, the Maghreb, and other Arab countries. Jews had lived in the Arab world in relative peace and harmony with their Muslim neighbors until the 1920s; when the first Arab revolts started in Palestine in 1929, they claimed more than one hundred Jewish victims. As a result, Jews started to attack Arabs.

Most clashes took place in Jaffa, which was almost entirely destroyed, and in different neighborhoods in Jerusalem. During the Hebron Massacre, the city's entire Jewish population was wiped out after they had lived in the city for many generations. Jews attacked and destroyed Arab villages in retaliation, killing all their inhabitants. A political power vacuum took hold of Palestine immediately—a disaster for the Palestinians who were left without any leaders.

The Big Arab Revolt of 1936-1939

After the National Socialist regime came to power in Germany in 1933 and invaded many parts of Europe, Jews started to seek a safe haven in Palestine in greater numbers, as most countries had closed their borders to them.

As one of the results of this mass immigration, and after a period of relative calm, Arab attacks began again in 1936. They lasted until 1939, causing great bloodshed among Jews and Arabs. A full-scale national uprising set in. At the beginning of World War II, immigration came to a halt, greatly impacting the Middle East: firstly, because the colonial powers were involved in the war against Germany and Italy; secondly, because many Jews were fleeing from Europe to Palestine legally and illegally.

In 1936, the Arab riots escalated into a large revolt, not least because of the hesitation of the British government to sort out the Arab-Jewish conflict. On the one hand, the British felt an obligation towards both sides, on the other, the geopolitical situation had changed completely with Hitler's rise to power in Germany. The threat of a new World War was written on the wall. These riots lasted from 1936 to 1939 and went on almost without interruption.[88] Simultaneously, the Jewish Yishuv erected fifty-two new agricultural border settlements, which, according to existing Ottoman law, could not be destroyed as long as they had a roof.

Antisemitism started to spread in the Arab world, with the Muslim Brothers demonstrating in Egypt against the Jews, and a massacre in Baghdad, which together caused most Jews to leave the Arab countries. They could no longer call themselves Iraqi Jews or Egyptian Jews and stay in the land they had lived in for hundreds of years.

Husseini, the Mufti of Jerusalem, was banned from Palestine. He then went to Germany and tried to recruit Arab soldiers for the Nazi army, but succeeded only in Bosnia.[89]

Fifth Aliyah

The Fifth Aliyah to Palestine occurred between 1933 and 1939. It was neither planned nor intended. Not many Jews chose to come to Palestine willingly, but rather for lack of other options. The world did not want to receive Jewish refugees, who were often refused a visa to other countries.[90] This aliyah originated in Hitler's Germany after he seized power, and it was a question of life or death for Jews. In order not to end up in concentration or death camps, Jews had to leave Europe. They started to escape from Germany in 1933, and from Austria, Poland, the Czech Republic, Ukraine, Italy, Belgium, France, and the Southern Balkan from 1938 to 1939.[91]

Between 1933 and 1939, more than two hundred thousand Jews escaped from Europe, but not all of them went to Palestine.[92] The Olim wielded a big influence, especially on the development of Tel Aviv and Haifa, with both cities tripling in size. Jerusalem doubled in size. Jewish refugees brought modern machinery and industrial knowledge to the country, laying the foundation for an industrial sector. Many new jobs were created, mostly for Jews, but also for Arabs. In 1938, Jews made up 30 percent of the population of Palestine.[93] Ben Gavriel writes that between 1932 and 1935, around 140,000 European Jews made aliyah.[94]

Aliyat ha-No'ar - Youth Aliyah

Between 1932 and 1941, about 7,000 young people aged 6 to 18 from Germany and the German-occupied territories reached Palestine legally with the help of Youth Aliyah.[95] In comparison to other countries of immigration, this constituted the largest number of young people immigrating to any region in the world. The British government allowed their entrance, making an exception by not subjecting them to certificate restrictions. Most of them came without parents, and they were often the only ones in their families to survive the war.[96]

Aliyah Bet - Ha'apala[97]

The illegal immigration that took place until May 1948 is called Aliyah Bet or Ha'apala. About 80,000 Jews escaped Nazi persecution in Europe and came to Palestine from 1945 to 1948.[98] Since official emigration from Europe occurred side by side with illegal aliyah, it is impossible to know how many people entered the region from 1939 to 1948. Ben Gavriel writes that in the years 1946 and 1947, about 36 vessels managed to break the British blockade and enter Palestine illegally with roughly 43,500 refugees on board.[99]

Most Jews arrived in Palestine without any possessions and from 1939 onwards, were integrated by the Yishuv[100] in cities, villages and Kibbutzim with the help of the "Sohnut,"[101]—the Jewish Agency—as well as other Jewish and non-Jewish organizations, which were active mostly in London and the United States.

The Jews of Aliyah Bet largely belonged to the middle class. They included university graduates, physicians, artists, architects, scholars and teachers. They were to have a decisive influence on the development of Israeli sciences, arts, agriculture, civil engineering and the industrial sector.

British Commissions and Resolutions: 1937-1939

In 1937, the Peel Commission[102] came to a different conclusion about the situation in Palestine than previous commissions. After thoroughly researching the situation, the Peel Commission came to the conclusion that the only solution for Palestine was to divide the country and thereby create an Arab and a Jewish state, as it was obvious that the two groups of people could not live together.

In the wake of the Arab revolt, and just a few months before the onset of World War II, the British government issued a third White Paper in May of 1939. It was another attempt to solve the problems in Palestine, with which the British had hardly come to terms. It intended to create an independent "Palestinian state" in which a Jewish minority would maximally make up a third of the population and live within a restricted territory.[103]

The British Peel Commission[104] of 1937 realized that Britain's obligations to Arabs and Jews were irreconcilable and it therefore recommended, for the first time in history, the partition of Palestine into a Jewish independent state and a Palestinian autonomous territory that would join Transjordan. Although the Jewish state would have been a very small one, the Jewish leadership agreed to the plan and most Zionists worldwide followed them. Jerusalem was to be under British control and retain a passage to the Mediterranean Sea. These plans spurred on the Arab rebellion.[105] Both Arabs and Jews rejected all British efforts to solve the problem, and none of them were confident that the British were capable of solving the problem or willing to do so. The problems ceased when the threat of a new World War became obvious. In September 1939, World War II began—which was to change all plans.

1939 to 1947

During World War II and shortly thereafter, the Middle East was a very prosperous region. Agriculture and industry flourished. The "Keren Kayemet"[106] made maximum efforts to buy as much land as possible,[107] and from 1940 to 1947, Jewish land purchases measured 144,867 Dunams.[108]

The Mufti of Jerusalem, Hajj Amin al-Hussayni (1893-1974),[109] who had agitated against the British, was expelled from Palestine. He was pro-German and even visited Hitler in Germany during the war. The expulsion of al-Hussayni made space for other political movements, above all the Istiqlal.[110] The party acquired control of the Arab National Bank and the Arab National Fund and intended to buy land that might otherwise have been purchased by Zionists. Zionists were not the only rivals to the Istiqlal. Old and long-established clans such as the al-Nashashibis and the al-Hussaynis were still respected by local leaders and village elders. They knew that political turmoil was bad for business and tried to calm the young agitators.[111] "In 1941, a referendum initiated by the American consulate in Jerusalem and conducted by Halil Sakhanini, a Christian Palestinian, showed that 88 percent of Arabs were pro-German and 8 percent pro-Britain."[112]

During World War II, the Palestine Regiment was established. Around 33,000 Jews and about 9,000 Arabs joined the British forces voluntarily, but most Arabs soon deserted. This regiment was deployed on diverse fronts to perform ancillary services. The Jews wanted to participate in the fights against the Germans to which Prime Minister Winston Churchill agreed in 1944. Subsequently, a special Jewish brigade within the British army was established. This brigade fought on several fronts. A special parachutist troop did espionage work in Hungary, Yugoslavia, and Slovakia; half of them were captured and murdered by the Nazis.[113]

After the Cold War[114] started shortly after World War II, the United States and the Soviet Union started to wield more influence over the Middle East—with each country vying for hegemony in the region. This competition greatly affected the Middle East and was to shape the future of the entire region.

After World War II, 1945

After the end of the war in 1945, hundreds of thousands of Jews found themselves in camps for displaced persons all over Europe, as their countries of origin did everything to prevent their return. These countries were afraid that the Jews would demand what was taken away from them by force during the National Socialist regime. Most of the survivors did not even consider this possibility. All they wanted to do was get away from Europe. European governments were therefore content and relieved to get rid of the Jewish problem and to agree to a solution outside of Europe—which was obviously Palestine. It was Arabs of Palestine who had to pay the price.

A pan-Arab position was established at the Alexandria Conference of 1944. According to this position, Palestinian Arabs were the victims of World War II and could not be left without the support of their Arab brothers. In 1945, the Arab League was founded in Egypt with British support.

From an Arab point of view, it is true that without World War II and the murder of six million Jews, there would probably never have been such a strong movement of Jews from Europe to Palestine.[115] European governments were eagerly supporting the creation of the state of Israel as a homeland for the Jews; from that time on, the Jews stopped being a European problem and became a problem instead for the Palestinians and other Arabs of the Middle East.

The entire world, but first and foremost Europe, is responsible for the creation of the Jewish state. It should be said that neither a government in the West nor in the East thought about how this new state would affect the Arab inhabitants of Palestine.

"Israel is no longer the Jewish state created to save Jewish refugees from Europe. The concept of nationhood runs deep. For us, Judaism is not a nation but a religious concept,"[116] writes Yoram Kaniuk.

Since the United States enacted very restrictive immigration quotas between 1924 and 1948, large quantities of Jewish refugees went to Palestine. According to many experts, it is doubtful that the state of Israel would have been created without these restrictions. Most emigrants tried to go west, but ended up in the Middle East for lack of other options.[117]

The Partition Plan of 1947

In 1947, the British government was confronted with nationalist demands for independence from both Arabs and Jews and could therefore no longer cope with the situation in Palestine. As a result, Britain assigned the responsibility for Palestine to the United Nations. "In addition to being a new geopolitical statement, it was a purely moral-ethical statement... it was the payment of a debt by the countries that realized they could do better if they avoided the Jewish tragedy..."[118] Besides, American support for the foundation of a Jewish state became a matter of course after the Holocaust.[119] All this had happened at the expense of the Palestinian Arab population, which never had a say in the matter but was asked to pay the price.

Matters took a turn for the worse when Irgun, a right-wing paramilitary Jewish organization, attacked the Palestinian village of Dair Yasin and slaughtered its 115 inhabitants in 1948. This is how a never-ending dilemma of retaliation started. The Arabs responded by killing 70 doctors and nurses who were part of a medical convoy to Jerusalem. In a state of panic, over 300,000 Arabs had fled the region by May 15, 1948.[120] After the British government terminated its mandate in Palestine, responsibility for the region was turned over to the United General Assembly. The General Assembly adopted a recommendation to divide Palestine into an Arab state and a Jewish state and give the city of Jerusalem a special international status.[121] Jerusalem was to stay a separate entity, a "corpus separatum" under international law.[122]

The Jewish Point of View

The UN partition plan of 1947 would have been a strategic nightmare for the Jewish state: it would have consisted of a small district in East Galilee, another small district on the coast between Haifa and Tel Aviv, and parts of the Negev desert, with narrow points of intersection between the regions. The Jews agreed to this plan, but their Arab neighbors refused it. In 1948 they started a war against Israel, which in Israel today is called the "Independence War."

The Jewish leadership accepted the partition nevertheless. "That sacrifice (not to have Jerusalem as the capital of Israel) would be the Jewish contribution to the solution of a painful problem and would bear witness to the Jewish people's spirit of international cooperation and its desire for peace."[123] The United Nations General Assembly resolution of the partition was ratified by democratic vote on November 29, 1947, and welcomed by the Zionists, despite strategic and economic shortcomings.[124]

The Arab Point of View

The Arab Higher Committee vehemently rejected the proposal. "The Arabs bitterly opposed partition."[125] With the exception of Jordan, all Arab countries—especially the ones bordering on Israel—agreed to reject the partition.

According to Kraemer, it was important for Israel's Arab neighbors and rivals that Israel be prevented from acquiring more land than what they owned.[126] Israel's Arab population was just used as a pretext for the rejection of the partition. Each country was playing its own private game in order to obtain more influence and land and thus greater hegemony in the Middle East. The Arab League warned Europe not to solve the Jewish problem only by committing a bigger injustice against the Arabs of Eretz Israel.[127]

It was therefore not the Arab population of Palestine that instigated other Arab countries to take up arms against Israel. Instead, these countries were spurred on by their own desire for more influence. The destiny of the Palestinians was secondary to them, serving only as a pretext.

The Partition

On November 29, 1947, the General Assembly decided the partition of Palestine and voted on the establishment of a Jewish state—the state of Israel—within the territory of Palestine/Eretz Israel **(Map)**, and a Palestinian state. On May 15, 1948, the state of Israel was proclaimed. About 133,000 Palestinian Arab came under Israeli law.

But no matter what kind of partition was planned, the Arab population of Palestine never got its land. It was divided between Egypt in the South, Syria in the North, and Jordan in the East. Great Britain had given the West Bank to Jordan as early as 1922. It included the Palestinian population there, which became the majority of the Jordanian population.[128] Egypt was given the Gaza Strip in the southwest with all its Palestinian population, which numbered 350,000 people at the time.

"The partition of Palestine in 1947 was embraced by the Zionist community. After World War II and the Holocaust, with hundreds of thousands of Jews in Displaced Person Camps all over Europe, the European countries were relieved to get rid of the Jews by routing them to the Middle East."[129] This is probably one of the main reasons why the resolution was ratified by majority vote in the United Nations General Assembly.

The Partition led to a full-scale civil war. The Jews were now determined to establish their own state. The Haganah (later IDF) put into effect its D-Plan, which was conceived after Arab attacks on Jews. It sparked off of the Palestinian refugee problem in the region because it allowed for the deportation of (Muslim) civilians. This plan was the final stage of the Jews taking full possession of their country.

The Palestinians received help from some 3,000 volunteers from other Arab countries. "Tiberias, Haifa, Acre, Jaffa and much of the Arab part of Jerusalem fell into Jewish hands, and some three to four hundred thousand refugees streamed in terror towards the neighboring Arab countries."[130] The Jews made big gains in nearly all sectors that had been allotted to the Arabs.

The partition was ideal neither for Jews nor for Palestinian Arabs; both had to give up their dreams of taking into possession all of the land. A Palestinian mass exodus began. About 700,000 left Palestine, mostly for the East Bank, Gaza, and other Arab countries such as Jordan and Syria.[131]

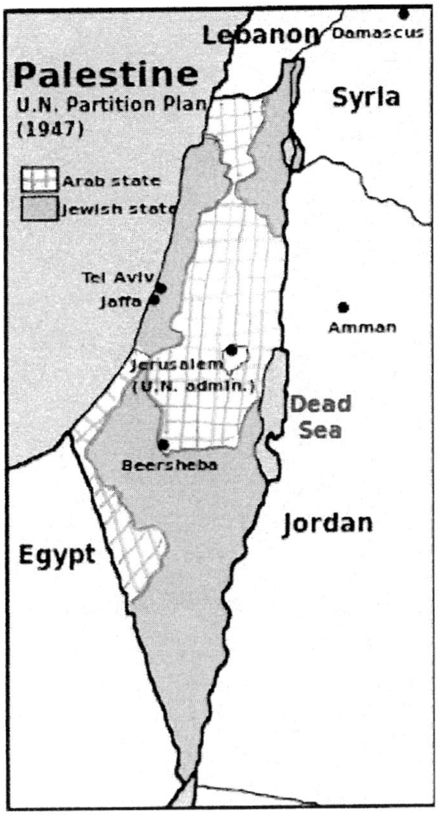
Palestine
U.N. Partition Plan
(1947)
Arab state
Jewish state
Lebanon
Damascus
Syria
Tel Aviv
Jaffa
Amman
Jerusalem
(U.N. admin.)
Dead
Sea
Beersheba
Jordan
Egypt

Civil War: November 1947 to May 1948

"There were no front lines and no territorial movements during the Civil War. The British did not get in the midst of Arabs and Jews, but tried—not very hard—to preserve a state of law and order until their mandate ended. At the beginning it looked like the Palestinians would be victorious because they had all the support from their Arab brothers, but disorganization and bad communication stood in their way."[132]

British troops tried to stop both Arab and Jewish aggression, but often arrived at the scene too late and with too little manpower. It seemed as if British troops were intervening only halfheartedly.

The end of the British Mandate in Palestine and the establishment of the Jewish state were the official reasons for the first Arab-Israeli War, which erupted on May 15, 1948. "The concern for the fate of European Jewry in the United States may have been an important factor ... for increased immigration into Palestine. ... When we think of who had the biggest interest in giving Jews a land of their own after the Holocaust, it is obvious that Europe had the biggest concern for solving the Jewish problem. After all, hundreds of thousands of Jews lived in displaced persons camps, and were in no position to decide where to go. European countries did not want them to return to their countries of origin. The United States was mostly concerned with the Cold War that started in the Middle East after World War II,"[133] writes Abu-Lughhod.

The Middle East, which had always been hurled between great powers, rose to greater prominence as the Cold War between the Soviet Union and the United States picked up steam. Soon, Israel became a reliable partner and a strategic asset for the United States. The Soviets counted Egypt and Syria as their allies.[134]

Fleeing from Palestine

The Arab countries did not accept the Partition plan, which was decided by the United Nations General Assembly on November 29, 1947 and subsequently incited the Palestinian to take up arms against the Jews. The Palestinians had not yet organized militarily and could only act in small groups with few weapons. A kind of Arab "army" started to penetrate Jewish cities, kibbutzim, villages, buses, and car convoys. The Israelis were much better organized and enormously motivated to fight back. They cleared Arab residential areas in Jerusalem, threatened and intimidated Arabs elsewhere, and demanded that Arabs abandon their homes.

The fleeing fever was infectious, causing about 75,000 Arabs—mostly from the urban upper and middle class—to leave the country. The Arab Higher Committee made desperate efforts to keep them back and even threatened to punish the ones who were leaving, but their efforts s hardly showed an effect. The Palestinian intelligentsia fled, and the peasant population had to face the enemy.[135]

Violence on both sides continued, with hundreds of Arab and Jewish casualties.[136] Some Palestinian leaders encouraged their people to leave, promising them a safe return after an impending Israeli defeat. As most of the Palestinian leaders were abroad, nobody believed them. Abu-Lughhod describes the situation differently in his book of essays: "Israeli forces surrounded and overwhelmed one Arab district after the other, so that most Palestinians fled beyond enemy lines."[137]

About 300,000 Palestinians from Jaffa, Haifa, Acre, Safed, and Tiberias fled the country before May 1948—half of the nearly 750,000 Palestinians who left the country between 1947 and 1949.[138]

Haganah assaults on major Arab centers such as Jaffa and Haifa—as well as expulsions carried out by right-wing groups such as Irgun Ezel,[139] Lehi or Stern—led to the exodus of large numbers of Arabs. Jewish atrocities and the escape of the Palestinian elite played an important role in the Palestinian exodus. Uri Avneri, a soldier in the War of 1948, described the conflict in an interview with *Haaretz* on November 2, 2013, as ethnic cleansing on both the Arab and the Israeli side.

Pre-War Period

At the end of 1947, "Arabs started to abandon Israel in masses because the Civil War posed a great threat to them, the economy had deteriorated, and Jewish markets were closed to Arab products. In addition, unemployment had risen to high levels, and the price of basic products had increased. Public transportation had stopped altogether."[140] "15,000 Arabs fled ... despite the mufti's call for them to stay and his request that Arab states refuse them entry,"[141] Cohen adds. Men between the ages of 16 and 60 were not allowed to enter neighboring countries because it was feared that they would start riots.

The Secretary-General of the Arab League—the confederation that included most Arab States—wrote in his cable to the UN Secretary-General on May 15, 1948:

"Now that the Mandate over Palestine has come to an end, leaving no legally constituted authority behind in order to administer law and order in the country and to afford the necessary and adequate protection to life and property, the Arab States declare as follows:

The right to set up a government in Palestine, referring to its inhabitants under the principles of self-determination recognized by the Covenant of the League of Nations, as well as the United Nations Charter.

The British administered Palestine after World War I, promising to establish a Jewish homeland. The original Mandate in Palestine included what became now Israel and the West Bank—Transjordan.[142] To the Palestinian people who view Palestine as their homeland, its borders are those of the Palestinian Mandate excluding Jordan, as manifested in the Palestinian National Charter."

Arab Countries against Israel

After years of Israeli rule, nothing catches more attention than burning the blue-white flag of Israel to remind everybody what the real evil is. It has become a tradition to flavor any Arabic campaign with a defamation of Israel—the only thing that the countries in the region agree upon.

"It is still possible to arrest and imprison people who speak out against the government in the Arab countries because these people supposedly undermine national feelings, encourage religious tensions, and offend the president of republics such as Syria or Iran,"[143] writes Hugi.

Moris writes that throughout their history, Palestinian Arabs have characteristically put the blame for their misery on others—the Ottomans, the British, Europe, the United States, the Jews, the United Nations, etc. When the Civil War started, most of the Palestinian

High Committee members stayed abroad because the Palestinians did not have enough weapons and ammunition to fight effectively, were not organized, and received no significant help from their Arab brothers. Very few young people from wealthy families took part in the war.[144]

Identity

Both Israelis and Palestinians were born as autochthonous identities on the same day: May 15, 1948—the day Israel was founded. The establishment of the state of Israel gave Arabs in the region a Palestinian identity and the Jews an Israeli identity. The only difference between Jews and Palestinians was that Jews became Israeli citizens right away, while Palestinians did not get a country of their own. They either left the region for Syria, Jordan, Egypt, Lebanon and other Arab countries as refugees or became citizens of Israel, the only country in which they were neither refugees nor exiles and are still defined as "Israeli Arabs."

"As they are interested in obtaining hegemony in the region, other Arab countries have made many decisions to 'help the Palestinians.' Instead of freeing Palestine, they each have annexed parts of it."[145] Ironically, the one who saw this coming ironically was Mufti el-Hussaini, who viewed all this help from Arab countries with great skepticism. The Mufti feared that Jordan, Syria, and Egypt would sideline the Palestinian problem and grasp the opportunity to "annex different regions."[146] He was right.

The War of 1948

Five Arab Countries Attack Israel

The real war between the Arab countries and Israel started after the proclamation of the state of Israel on May 15, 1948.[147] As of April 1948 the Arab armies of Egypt, Jordan, Syria, Lebanon and Iraq were preparing for a war against Israel and soon they entered

Palestine, which had been a British Mandate, and was now to be divided into two countries, Israel and Palestine.[148]

Except for Jordan, the Arab countries were ill-equipped and had 25,000 inefficient troops. Motivation ran low among them. The Israelis were better prepared. They had good logistics and communications systems as well as modern equipment and 35,000 troops that were highly motivated to fight for the state of Israel. (Those facts became evident to the Israeli and the Arab public much later.) The threat of the elimination of the state of Israel seemed insurmountable at the time. Compared to the small state of Israel with its 650,000 Jewish inhabitants and nascent institutions, Arab countries numbered millions of inhabitants. The Arabs were sure of their advantage and of a victory. The Israelis feared the confrontation but had no choice. David had to fight Goliath. Generations of Israelis were brought up with this narrative and had believed it for at least four decades; there was no reason to question it. Or so the story goes. When a group of New Historians in Israel questioned this narrative in the late 1980s, it began to crack.[149]

At the beginning, both Jews and Arabs believed that the Arab armies were stronger than the Israeli army. The Israeli military estimated their chance of winning as fifty-fifty. Both sides thought that there was one Israeli to two Arab soldiers, but that the Israelis were better equipped with artillery, tanks, infantry, and fighter aircraft.

By the end of the war the situation had changed dramatically. Israel bought a large amount of weapons on the black and grey market (mostly from Russia and Czechoslovakia), and the human resources situation was completely reversed. From April to November 1948, the Israeli army conquered more than 400 villages and cities, while Arab soldiers captured about 12 settlements.[150]

The only Arab leader to doubt an Arab triumph was King Abdullah of Jordan.

The majority of the Arab states viewed this conflict as a holy war against the infidels. “Jihad on behalf of Palestine was understood in terms of an apocalyptic prophecy.”[151]

The Palestine question united the Arabs like no other issue. Egypt, Jordan, Syria, Lebanon and Iraq wanted to free Palestine from the Jews and resettle Palestinian refugees back in their homeland, but in the end they were split because each one of them harbored their own territorial and hegemonic interests.[152] Although Egyptian president Gamal Abdel Nasser described the official reason for going to war against Israel as a desire to free Palestine, the Palestinians were forgotten by their Arab brothers, and soon these states ceased to mention the establishment of an independent Palestinian state altogether. In

Israel, this war is called the War of Independence: in Palestine, it has come to be known as *Nakhba*, the Catastrophe.

The Yishuv during the War

"The Yishuv pursued three goals during this war. First and foremost, they wanted to survive Arab attacks. Second, with the continuation of the war, it was decided to expand the territory beyond the borders of the partition so Israel would obtain defendable borders. Third, the army was tasked with reducing the hostile Arab minority inside Israel either by fighting them or by expelling them from the country."[153]

Both for Israel and the Arab enemy, the annexation of territories beyond the suggested partition borders was one of the most important results of this first Arab-Israeli war.[154]

During the War of 1948, 6,000 Israeli soldiers and civilians were killed—1 percent of Israel's Jewish population. The small, new state of Israel was confronted with five enemies. This is a historical fact. Only much later, when Israeli archives were opened, was it possible to analyze the real dimension of historical events. Without a doubt, Jewish fighters fought heroically—until the first truce in smaller numbers and with fewer weapons than Arab soldiers. When the Israeli army increased its weapons and ammunition stockpile and trained more soldiers after the first truce, it counted about 100,000 troops by December 1948—many more than all Arab enemy armies combined.

The fact that every single Arab country pursued its own dynastical and political interests is probably one of the most important reasons why the Arab coalition lost the war. Israel annexed larger territories than those ceded to it in the UN partition plan.[155] The other parts of Palestine—the West Bank, the Gaza Strip and the Golan Heights— were annexed by Arab countries bordering on these territories. During talks with Jordan from 1948 to 1951[156] and later on with Egypt and Jordan, neither country ever mentioned the creation of a Palestinian state after an Israeli withdrawal.

After the War of 1948

In February 1949, Jordan, Syria, Lebanon and Egypt signed a truce with Israel and for the following twenty years the creation of a Palestinian state was never mentioned again. Israel was to sign a separate peace agreement with each one of its rivals. The Gaza Strip was occupied by Egypt and the West Bank came under Jordanian rule. Jordan also annexed the old city of Jerusalem.

From 1949 to 1964 the Palestinians were absent as an independent political power in the Middle Eastern arena, partly because they were divided across political and ideological lines, partly because the Arab countries wanted to have the Palestinians in their hands and so suppressed any Palestinian independence efforts.[157]

As a result of the Arab-Israeli War of 1948, Israel captured and incorporated an additional 26 percent of the Mandate territory (in addition to the territories, it was accorded in the Partition Plan). "The creation of the state of Israel was a personal affront for each single Arab. The biggest problem of losing the War of 1948 was the humiliation the Arabs felt and still feel."[158] In Arab society, honor plays a much bigger role than in other civilizations. An Arab will never excuse his assault until the other side takes revenge.

The War of 1948 was a break-even point between two national movements—but it was also part of a global struggle between the Arab world and Europe, in which Israel has been the most important battlefield, as the country is viewed by the Arabs to be an extension of colonial regimes. This makes the Middle East probably the biggest clash of civilizations in the world. This status quo has enabled Israel to overpower a coalition of Arab societies, which were stronger demographically and bigger geopolitically.[159]

"If the Arab countries had not initiated the war against Israel, the Palestinian-Arabs would have stayed in their homes and we would not have banished them. The state of Israel would have a completely different demographic concept,"[160] Israeli Minister Moshe Sharet said many years later.

Occupied Territories

Since 1948, Palestinian territories have been occupied by Egypt, Jordan, Syria, or by Israel. The occupation did not start—as is commonly believed—in 1967, but in 1948 by the three above-mentioned Arab countries. "In the Arab world alone, each state or government deems it necessary to assure itself of some sort of influence, proxy voice, or interference in Palestinian politics. Through the Palestinian connection, these governments maintain legitimacy and authority. At times this resulted even in bloodshed,"[161] writes Edward Said.

"After the War of 1948, the Arab countries demanded that Israel should go back to the borders agreed on in the UN Partition Plan of November 29, 1947. The Israeli delegation to the talks retorted that it could not agree to these borders, as the Arab countries had not accepted the partition in the first place, and under these new circumstances Israel would not withdraw from its position."[162] Israel considered the newly won territories and new borders a better guarantee for its security.

"If it had not been for the Arab-initiated War of 1948 ... it is impossible to imagine that Israel would have initiated a mass expulsion of Arabs with hundreds of thousands of Arabs fleeing. ... By the end of the war, about 78 percent of the Mandate territory of Palestine came under Israeli control,"[163] Abu-Lughhod writes. "After 1948, the Jewish military authorities occupied properties and turned them over to Jews by putting them under the 'absentee' laws."[164] This is a fact known by everyone in Israel.

Demography[165]

The following section draws on census data and official documents to present a demographic history of the Jewish and Arab populations in Palestine, Israel and the Palestinian territories.

Palestine:

1936:	400,000 Jews;	800,000 Arabs
1947:	630,000 Jews;	1,310,000 Arabs

UN Partition Plan (1947):

Jewish State:	498,000 Jews;	407,000 Arabs
Arab State:	725,000 Arabs;	10,000 Jews

Israel:

1949:	1,013,000 Jews;	159,000 Arabs

The decrease in the Arab population between 1947 and 1949 is due to the Palestinian exodus of 1948.

The Aftermath, the Refugees

Who is a Refugee?

Refugees are people who live outside of their native countries, in a place they cannot or are not allowed to call home—in a country that does not accept them as equals and does not give them any political or human rights. Mostly it is a temporary circumstance, which ends with either integration or deportation.

Palestinian Refugees in Arab countries

The journalist Eskin Childers writes that over the last few years many scholars—Jews and non-Jews, Zionist and non-Zionist alike—have asserted that before April 1948 there was no evidence of Jews wanting to drive the Arabs out of the region. Indeed, only some 30,000 Palestinians left, the majority of them being middle and upper class. These people were regarded as traitors by the ones who stayed behind. Some Israeli historians have claimed that this move lowered Arab morale and contributed to the ensuing mass exodus. Arab leaders tried to stop the exodus by speaking on the radio, distributing leaflets and even by threatening the ones who left, but without success. "They left in great panic and left disorder behind."[166]

Around 700,000 Palestinians fled or were expelled from the area that became Israel after the War of 1948, and were not allowed to return. About 133,000 Palestinians remained in Israel. Of the ones who left, about 470,000 went into refugee camps in Jordan, in Jordan-Palestine (the West Bank), and in Egypt-Palestine (the Gaza Strip). The rest was dispersed in Lebanon, Syria, and some refugees chose more remote destinations in Arab countries and outside the Middle East. The problem was that they were ... often the pawn of Arab states rivalries."[167] They became refugees, a status most of the Palestinians in Arab countries remain forced into even today. They are supported by the United Nations organization such as United Nations Relief and Works Agency for Palestine Refugees in the Near East (UNRWA). Palestinian refugees have not been allowed to return to Israel nor have they been granted citizenship or human rights in the Arab countries.

The fact that Palestinians in the Arab countries consider themselves refugees after more than sixty years is an exception worldwide. It shows that something went wrong with the Palestinians in those countries. Still, according to Hadawi, only the Jews are to be blamed, not the Arab brotherhood. He seems to hate Israel and does not shy away from making accusations in order to strengthen his arguments. He makes his arguments without giving evidence. This does not mean that he is lying, but he is not saying the truth when he accuses Israel of planning to expel all Palestinian inhabitants from its territories and suggests "the total destruction of the state of Israel" as a response.

Israeli Arabs

The Israeli army captured and incorporated a further 26 percent of the Mandate territory; Jordan acquired the region today known as the West Bank from the British authorities as early as 1922. Egypt occupied the Gaza Strip in 1948.

The Palestinian Arab population that remained in what became Israel after the war was granted Israeli citizenship. Arab Israelis were subject to martial law until 1966, at which time security restrictions placed on Arab citizens of Israel were lifted completely, and they were theoretically granted the same rights as Jewish citizens, although they are discriminated against in many ways—on the job market, in housing, etc.

"There are no words to describe the appalling tragedy of the Arab refugees and the conditions in which they live,"[168] writes Nasser about Palestinians in Arab countries.

The question remains why Palestinians in Arab countries are still refugees and why they still have to live in camps. Why did the Arab countries not do anything to redress this situation if Palestinians are their brothers? Why have Palestinians not been treated as equals or granted citizenship in Arab countries? What has happened to basic human empathy for these poor Palestinian brothers who are still stuck in camps?

By no means can it be the fault of the Palestinians themselves or their inability to run their own lives. Research on the subject has shown that they are doing very well in countries outside the Middle East as well as in Israel. Who else is therefore to blame for their eternal refugee status, if not their Arab brothers?

"... Here they stand, the victims of an international conspiracy."[169] With the exception of Jordan, most of the Arab states have denied citizenship to Palestinian refugees to this day. Lebanon refused to give citizenship to about 250,000 Palestinians even they had lived in the country as refugees for dozens of years.

Palestinians outside of the Middle East

The Palestinians I met in Europe, the United States and outside the Middle East understand the refugee problem, but most would never fight for Palestine because it is an abstract place for them. Almost all of them would not consider living there. They are

Americans, British etc. The generations who were born in other countries have very little in common with the Middle East and its problems, and Palestine is a place they have heard stories about from their grandparents.
Like Jewish refugees throughout the course of history, they have integrated in their new countries and identify with these nations.
Although many would identify their origins as Palestinian, they left behind their refugee status a long time ago, as it is the case with all other immigrants in the free world.

Jewish Refugees

Jews from Arab countries suffered a similar fate as the Palestinians. Half of about one million Jews from Arab countries immigrated to Israel. As a result of physical and political insecurity posed by the Arab–Israeli War of 1948, about one million Jews fled or were expelled from their homes in all Arab countries, with the majority being forced to abandon their property. 260,000 of them reached Israel from 1948 to 1951. 600,000 arrived in the country by 1972. Jews from Arab countries were murdered and expelled—in addition to having their property confiscated—in Aden, Haleb, Pakistan, Iran, Bahrain, Egypt, Iraq, Beirut, Tripoli, and the Maghreb. As there were refugees on both sides, it became a dual problem.[170] The difference between Jewish refugees and Palestinian refugees is that soon after their arrival in Israel, Jews were not counted as refugees. They were granted citizenship and became Israelis. Wherever they went, they were able to start a new life and to become citizens, as was the case with Palestinians outside the Arab world.

Why Palestinians Remain Refugees

Benni Moris writes that among many reasons for this Arab attitude of neglect, some Arab countries understood perfectly well that Palestinian refugees would eventually constitute a pool of guerilla fighters that could always be mobilized against Israel.[171]

The Palestinian Authority claims that people who fled their homes because their lives were threatened in conflicts such as the War of 1948 should have the right to return. In the process, the Palestinian Authority forgets that many of the refugees or former refugees do not even consider returning to Palestine.

On July 19, 1957, Radio Cairo pronounced that "the refugees are the cornerstone of the Arabic struggle against Israel. The refugees are the weapons of the Arabs and of the Arab nationality." And indeed, Arab countries that shelter Palestinian refugees behave according to this doctrine.

In an article written in 1976, Mahmud Abbas—head of Fatah, since 2005 President of the Palestinian Authority in the West Bank—proclaimed: "The Arab armies entered Eretz Israel with the purpose of protecting Palestinians from Zionist aggression. Instead, they abandoned them, forcing them to emigrate and leave their homeland, imposing a political quarantine on them and throwing them into ghettos. ... The Arab countries succeeded in dispersing the Palestinians and in destroying their unity. ... They never recognized them as a nation until other countries did."[172] This situation started after Israel invaded the territories in 1967, which enabled Palestinians to start a national movement.

Most Palestinians who live outside the Western world—and I have spoken with quite a few—not only don't want to return or, in the case of the second and third generations, move to Palestine. People who were born in the host countries call themselves American, French, British, of Palestinian origin. They told me that they went to Palestine for a visit, but did not consider it their country. They also said that their grandparents might give me a different answer.

Israel Is Blamed

Nasser writes that Jews are to blame for all the misery that Palestinians have experienced, because they have prevented them from obtaining healthcare and an education.[173] By contrast, when Israeli Arabs are interviewed in the media and are asked if they would move to a Palestinian state once it is established, they unequivocally reject the idea, even though they have not yet obtained equal rights in Israel. Said writes, "Torture of Arabs is a regular, methodical, and officially sanctioned device in Israel." and "the state of Israel condones the practice as a way of intimidating, controlling, and terrorizing the 'native' population in the Occupied Territories."[174] This is unfortunately true in too many cases. In my interviews with Arab-Israeli citizens, however, I heard statements such as "Do not to call me Palestinian. These are the troublemakers in the territories. I'm an Arab–Israeli. I'll never go to live in Palestine because although I have problems with the authorities, I still live in a democracy in Israel and this is not likely to happen there."[175]

Goitein comment in the following way on this subject, "There is no need to mince words about the demographic and economic prosperity of the Arabs in Israel. Anyone who visited Arab villages a generation ago is now struck by the tremendous progress."[176]

Refugees and Absentees

Very soon after the partition was decided in 1947, Jews realized that they should not rely on the United Nations to enforce their plans. A state of panic combined with terror attacks on both sides resulted in an exodus of over 300,000 Arabs on May 15, 1948.[177]

Israel proclaimed that Arabs who left—partly after being encouraged by Arab leaders or Israeli authorities—did not count as refugees, and therefore had no right to return. The Israeli government declared their property public and the refugees were counted as "absentees."[178] Arab property was expropriated from individuals as well as from entire villages and leased to Israelis and Jewish newcomers. In 1953, a new law of compensation for land taken by Israel came into force.

The land that became part of the state of Israel was mostly bought by the Keren Kayemet and by private Jewish investors. The land of the Palestinians who left or were expelled was confiscated. "Compensation was not paid. 750,000 refugees never came home to claim their possessions."[179] Exactly the same happened to Jews from the Arab countries.

The property the Palestinians left behind was called "absentee property" or "abandoned property" and was confiscated by the Israeli government. In 1954 it included big territories of agricultural land; about 8,700 dunam of agricultural area, and about 150 dunam of urban area as well as buildings, mostly in the cities. All this property was in the hands of the Israeli government and until today is leased out. It has not become private property.[180]

Religious Groups

Adding to all this acrimony, the presence of orthodox and ultra-orthodox Jews in Jerusalem and elsewhere led to malicious exchanges between the two. Non-religious Jews were assaulted by orthodox and ultra-orthodox Jews. Garbage from Yeshiva schools was thrown at them and they have been called Nazis.

Just like fundamentalist groups in the Arab world, Orthodox Jews have advocated for a religious Jewish state and for imposing Jewish biblical law on Israel, even though they have always been a small minority. Orthodox and ultra-orthodox Jews have not yet succeeded because Israel was built on Zionist secular ideology, which did not want the "Diaspora Jew" from Europe to become the image of Israel, a country that saw itself as being inhabited by "new, free Jews."[181] Neturei-Karta, the most fanatic Jewish religious group, even claims that all of Palestine should come under Palestinian rule because Jews do not have a claim to the country as long as the Messiah has not arrived.

Trying to Solve the Palestinian Problem

In 1949, Israel offered members of families separated by the War of 1948 a right of safe return. Israel also offered to repatriate 100,000 of the Palestinian refugees and to reopen refugee accounts that had been frozen in Israeli banks. The Arab states rejected this offer because they were unwilling to take any action that might be understood as a recognition of Israel. And as usual, the Arabs did not have Palestinian interests at heart.[182]

After the War of 1948 ended, most of the Palestinian refugees lived in camps in the West Bank within Jordanian-controlled territory; in the Gaza Strip, which became part of Egypt and was as a whole a refugee camp; and in Syria, Lebanon, Jordan and other places. Under Prime Minister David Ben-Gurion, the Israeli government's position was that Israel would pay the refugees compensation. This was not accepted as a solution by the Arab states. At the time, Israel focused on first settling and integrating Jewish refugees from Europe, and later those from the Arab countries.

In February of 1949, Jordan, Syria, Lebanon and Egypt signed separate armistice agreements with Israel, but the war never really ended.

Arab countries refused to integrate Palestinian refugees. That is why to this day, the Palestinian refugee problem has not been solved. Many Palestinian refugees still live in camps in Beirut, Damascus, Amman, and Nablus and have depended on support from the United Nations Organization for the Relief of the Palestinians (UNRWA) [183] and other UN organizations for more than 60 years. UNRWA had a budget of US$233 million in 1988. More than half of it came from the USA, supposedly "the big enemy of the Palestinians" and from Western Europe. Arab countries supported Palestinian refugees with a total of US$18 million.[184] Interestingly, most refugees are blaming the United States for their misery. Inexplicably, they have never blamed Europe, the Soviet Union, or the Arab countries for their plight.

The idea that UNRWA aid to the Palestinians means recognition of their status[185] might be correct, but if so, it could also be viewed as a case of bad conscience towards the Palestinians on the part of the United Nations; this permanent aid has made the Palestinians in the refugee camps depend on donations for more than 65 years. This is a very long time. Many Palestinians have become apathetic and unable to take their lives and destiny into their own hands, obtain an education, work, or do anything productive. To consider this status quo a given fact puts them in a position without obligations for themselves, and so they have retained the status of refugees. This is a mistake, as there are many exceptions among them that prove that it is possible to act differently.

After May 15, 1948

After the establishment of the state of Israel on May 15, 1948, more than 700,000 Jews came to Israel from all over the world. Israel's Jewish population more than doubled within two years. It was not only European Jews who immigrated, but also many Jews from Arab countries who had either been expelled from or left the region because their living conditions had deteriorated and they understood that they had no future in these countries.[186]

European Jews—survivors of the Holocaust—often came from Displaced Persons Camps that had been established by the Allies for survivors of Nazi concentration and death camps.[187] With the establishment of the state of Israel, these survivors had the chance to immigrate to the region, which was closed to them during the British Mandate. "By closing the borders hermetically to anybody, Britain stood like a wall between the displaced persons who were Jewish refugees and the Promised Land."[188]

The state of Israel after the War of 1948 (white) Size: 20,000 square kilometers
Territories occupied by Jordan, Syria and Egypt until the 1967 war (diagonal lines)

Talks between Israel and the Arab countries were held in Lausanne, Switzerland from April to September 1949. They ended in a fiasco. The Arab states wanted Israel to withdraw within the partition borders, which they themselves had not accepted in 1947. They demanded more territorial space for themselves, but did not pursue their goal of establishing a Palestinian state as they had originally claimed.[189]

After the disaster of 1948, the Arab League decided to impose an economic boycott on Israel. The Arab countries also boycotted countries that did not follow the Arab boycott and instead continued to deal with Israel. This situation reached a climax in 1951, when Arab countries boycotted some 8,500 companies around the world—among them Ford and Coca Cola—in an attempt to force Israel to its knees. These measures had some impact on Israel, but in the long run did not succeed in isolating the country.[190]

The Arab Neighbors

"Palestinians living in other Arab states, within Arab communities, felt deprived and discriminated against on a psychological and social level and frustrated about the way Arab leaders were addressing the conflict with Israel on an international level. Palestinians were disappointed about the help they received from their Arab brothers (...) As they were discriminated against in different Arab countries, Palestinians started to develop a Palestinian identity, which prevented them from integrating in Arab societies,"[191] writes Steinberg.

If we look at what happened after May 1948, we may wonder why the Arab countries started a war against Israel in the first place. Israelis and the Palestinians both seemed to accept the partition. Israel had just been founded and accepted the partition because it was obvious that there was no other possibility. Palestinians had not yet formed a concept of nationhood; they were not asked whether they agreed to the partition plan, and they did not even ask for help or advice from their Arab brothers. They just kept quiet. Why did the war start then, and on whose behalf and in whose interest was it waged? It did not take place in the interest of Israel or the Palestinians: neither party wanted the war, although both became victims of it.

The argument that Palestinian Arabs were not content with the partition is most probably true—as also applies to the Israeli Jews—though the war actually took place between the Arab world and Israel. It was not about conquering territories for a Palestinian state, but rather about the Jews as an alien element in the Middle East, which the Arab countries did not want to let exist, as they considered Palestine an Arabic-Islamic territory. The other reason for the war was Arab greed for more land as well as a bigger role in the world than their Arab brothers. This war was always about hegemony and honor in the Middle East, never about the rights of the Palestinians or a Palestinian state.

Starting in May of 1948, Israel's Arab neighbors started a campaign to stop the influx of Palestinian refugees from Israel into their territories by trying to convince them to return. Egypt prohibited any Palestinian who was able to carry a weapon from entering its territory. Lebanon and Syria prohibited the immigration of men between the ages of sixteen and sixty. These measures did not work because the Arab countries were not able to patrol and protect their borders as they were waging a war against Israel.[192]

When the war ended with a ceasefire in January of 1949, only 21 percent of Palestine remained in Arab hands, but never became a Palestinian state. The Gaza Strip came under Egyptian occupation, the West Bank under Jordanian, and the Golan Heights under Syrian. The idea of a Palestinian state was put aside and no Palestinian ever addressed the matter again as long as these territories were occupied by Arab states (i.e. until the War of 1967).

A Palestinian State

It may not have been on a conscious level, but the Palestinian people realized in 1948 that their Arab brothers who had come to their aid against the Israelis were not thinking about establishing a Palestinian state. Palestinians also knew that their hands were tied because they lived in these countries as disenfranchised refugees. Only much later did they realize that these countries acted solely in their own interests and not in the interests of the Palestinians, but by then it was too late to change the situation. In 1948, borders were drawn between Israel and its Arab neighbors, and none of these countries considered the Palestinians an equitable partner.

As Israel reluctantly agreed to the partition, the Palestinian did nothing. The Arab countries surrounding Israel did not accept the partition and started the war against Israel in 1948 on behalf of the Palestinian people. As the Arab countries had been insincere in their efforts to help the Palestinians, why should Israel give back land after winning the war?

Would the Arab countries accept the partition or would they start yet another war against Israel that would completely change the national composition of the Middle East? The Palestinians did not seem to have any part in the War of 1948, and neither were they involved in the Wars of 1956, 1967, and 1973. It is safe to assume that the Arab countries wanted Palestine for themselves—not for the purpose of creating a Palestinian state.

Hadawi insists that Israel did not want to accommodate the other countries, although in his opinion it should have. Nobody can imagine what would have happened to the Jews in Israel if the Arabs had won this war—after all, the Arabs declared that they would throw all the Jews into the sea if they emerged victorious. The Arab countries would have never created a Palestinian state, as they in fact failed to do for twenty years. Hadawi also writes that solutions have been proposed, but they have always ignored the Palestinians' right to their country. The Arab invaders pretended to consider this question at the time, but not one of them—Egypt, Jordan or Syria—wanted to renounce their right to the territories.

The Palestinians had to wait until they came under Israeli occupation in 1967 to start thinking about and fighting for a state of their own. These considerations became possible only under Israeli rule.

"Because their longing for Palestine was so deep, they could not imagine staying in another country,"[193] writes Hadawi, and puts the blame of not having integrated in the Arab countries on the Palestinians alone. This is partially correct, but the main reason for this non-integration is that the Arabs did not let Palestinians forget where they belonged. Jordan, Egypt, and Syria made sure Palestinians never felt welcome in their territory, constantly reminding them that they had no rights and that were only allowed to stay because of the "good will" and "generosity" of their hosts.

As Palestinians still live in the refugee camps in miserable conditions, it is only natural that they long for their lost homeland. This only applies to Palestinians who live in the Arab world, however. Those who left for other continents are well integrated because they were given the opportunity to settle down and make a life for themselves.

The Arab Trauma

Hans Benedict, a veteran correspondent for Austrian media in the Middle East, writes, "The Arabs suffer from a trauma because they lost a war against Israel. This war, in turn, sparked the Palestinian refugee tragedy. All forthcoming generations could not accept their status as stateless and disenfranchised refugees who lived in social isolation in camps in various Arab countries ... they [the Palestinians] wanted 'Palestine' instead of Israel. ... It also became obvious that the Arab hosts do not act like brothers towards the Palestinian refugees because they fear that they might turn into dangerous revolutionaries. The Palestinian refugees found themselves among people that by pure chance spoke Arabic but did not want to have anything to do with them. They were stuck into ghetto-camps were many live to this day. In no country in the Western world have the Palestinians suffered as much they have in Arab countries. In Europe and the United States there are large minorities of Palestinians that are well-integrated, well educated, and would never consider returning to Palestine, let alone their children who were born there."[194]

A typical paradox of the Middle East is that the PLO can argue its case better with Israel than with the Arab countries. There are many Palestinian newspapers and magazines, as well as a news and information service for foreign correspondents and for the Israeli media in the Occupied Territories and in Israel. In the Arab countries, there is almost a total lack of a free Palestinian press, except for one journal in Cairo and some irregular publications that toe the government line.[195]

The Palestinians had to pay the price for Arab megalomania, which started in 1948 with the war against Israel. Together with Israel, Palestinians have become the long-time losers in this conflict. "In Gaza the population was stateless and disenfranchised under Egyptian occupation. The Egyptian government did not have any ambition to annex this 'agitated, uneasy, overcrowded, overpopulated and visibly impoverished population and the territory of Gaza."[196]

Martial Law

By 1950, Israel faced the problem of having an Arab/Muslim population of about 170,000 that was considered a potential "fifth column" in spite of its status as Israeli citizens. Israel could not estimate where the loyalty of these Arab Muslims lay, and therefore placed most of them into designated military zones outside the reaches of civil law. Arab Israelis could be banished, and have their property confiscated; entire villages were moved if the security forces considered them a threat to particular locations.[197] Under this law, houses and land were taken away from their owners if the Israeli military authorities thought they needed this real estate for military purposes or for the security of Israeli citizens. Security and safety have always been sacred cows in Israel, and for years nobody criticized these confiscations. The Israeli military was able to act freely, and almost nobody objected to its actions.

"For nearly a decade, until 1958, the Palestinians remained passive towards their fate," writes Abu-Lughhod.[198] The Palestinians in fact remained this way until 1967 when they came under Israeli occupation.

Palestinian refugees aroused suspicion not only in Israel, but also in most Arab countries. Until 1950, UNRWA was the only organization to support them. They were mostly confined to overcrowded refugee camps and restricted in their movements in Gaza and West Jordan as well as in Jordan, Lebanon, Syria, and other Arab countries. Israel insisted that Arab countries receive them just like Israel had received Jews from the Arab world.

A solution was not in the interest of the Arab countries. Palestinian refugees have remained in refugee camps in the Arab world from 1948 until today. Despite martial law, the Palestinians who stayed in Israel were never confined to refugee camps but stayed in their cities and villages.

The Suez/Sinai War of 1956

In June 1956, the British ended their occupation of Egypt and left the country. Gamal Abdel Nasser (1918-1970, *de facto* president of Egypt from 1954 to 1970) nationalized the Suez Canal on July 26, 1956, preventing Israeli ships from entering the Gulf of Aqaba and the canal.[199] As a result, the French and British decided to start a war against Egypt, with Israel as their henchman. Israel was supposed to start the war so the French and the British would have a pretext to reoccupy the canal. The United States and the Soviet Union opposed this plan.

On October 29, 1956, the Israeli infantry, air force and navy started a war against Egypt. Nasser responded by sinking 40 Israeli ships in the Suez Canal and blockading it until early 1957. The Israeli army reached the West Bank of the Suez Canal, destroying 200 airplanes of the Egyptian air force and killing some 2000 to 3000 Egyptians. French and British forces subsequently started to bomb Cairo. After pressure from the United Nations, United States and the Soviet Union, the Anglo-French forces withdrew before the end of the year. Israel stayed in Egypt until March 1957, after it attained free passage through the Straits of Tiran. UN troops were sent to the Egyptian-Israeli border to prevent hostilities on both sides.[200]

This was the only war in the Middle East in which Israel attacked an Arab country, and it was the only war that was waged solely between Egypt and Israel. Neither the Palestinians nor the other Arab countries got involved in this war. Egyptian feelings of hatred against Israel were rekindled because of an injured collective ego.

Conflicting Interests

As mentioned before, the Arab world was never interested in establishing a Palestinian state. “Locked in a struggle for influence on Arab public opinion, Iraq and Egypt were equally vehement in their rhetoric about upholding Arab rights in Palestine.” Inter-Arab rivalries and disunity involved all four neighbors of Israel plus Iraq. It was the issue of hegemony in the Middle East as well as their concern for maintaining a balance between radicals and traditionalists that motivated the Arab countries. “When Arabs feel like cooperating, they usually agree to avoid taking action on Palestine. But when they choose to quarrel, Palestine policy readily becomes a subject of dispute,”[201] writes Abu-Lughhod. The Arab countries have never put up a united front in a war for Palestinian independence and have never agreed even on the question of Israel, their most beloved enemy. Instead, each country has followed its own interests in acquiring a piece of former Palestine for itself. The Palestinian problem never fostered unity in the Arab world by which different countries would put their respective interests aside and stop their rivalries.[202]

It was more complicated than that. It was "the wish of the Palestinians to eliminate Israel and to establish a secular, democratic state of Palestine, which differed from the ambiguous, multiple, and contradictory goals of various Arab regimes."[203] There was a feeling that a Palestinian solution would not only be a disservice to the interests of the Arab countries, but that a Palestinian state would become the first Arab democracy and thus threaten the other Arab countries. Arab states feared the ripple effect a Palestinian democracy would have, "What if there is a democratic country in the Arab world and all other Arabs wanted to have democracy as well?"

The Palestinian Problem

When Palestinians fled the region, the Arab countries had to deal with hundreds of thousands of penniless and homeless Arabs. It was not in their interest to integrate these people and to support them. They simply did not want them, but could not stop the influx—they were occupied with the war against Israel and did not have enough military power to simultaneously wage war and keep the fleeing Palestinians away.

Palestinians suffered the same fate as Jews after World War II—no country in the world wanted them. Instead of taking care of their Palestinian brothers and sisters, Arab countries provoked a war against Israel. The idea that the Arab countries went to war in order to protect their Palestinian brothers and sisters is an illusion. They just wanted the Palestinians to stay where they were.[204] "The Arab refugees ... are the symbol of the paramount political issue in the Middle East. Their plight is the direct outgrowth of an armed struggle between Arabs and Israelis."[205] "Not even God can change the past," wrote the Greek philosopher Agathon (448-400 BCE).

Israelis and Palestinians

Differences and Similarities

"We are what we know...The more we understand, the more human we are,"[206] writes William Chittick. From an ethical point of view, both Israelis and Palestinians should have a value system in which the equality of human beings ranks supreme. Unfortunately, this is not the case in this conflict. Both parties are entangled in a "cultural conflict" that they obviously have not been able to overcome because it is an integral part of their identity and national narrative. The question is not whether Israel and the Palestinians want peace or not because peace is a matter of survival for both people. In the six-decade-long conflict both are victims and perpetrators at the same time. Both parties to the conflict do not trust each other. And how could it they? Trust, however, is essential to their survival or elimination, to life or death. Trust is not something a government can decide to impose upon its people. It is a process that needs to be built over many years. As long as the process does not start, it cannot develop; and it starts with a peace agreement.

Chittick writes, [207] "Just like the West and the East on a whole, the Palestinian and the Israeli society have widely different cultures and traditions:

For Arabs, the most essential and indispensable part of being a Muslim is respect. Symbolism, myths and legends play an important role in their culture. The notion of family also includes the extended family. Arabs place great value on other people's opinion of them and their actions. They also cherish the motto, 'swiftness is from Satan.'"

Israelis, by contrast, are bound together by tradition and history, not by religion. This tradition is the basis of an atheistic society. They value rationalism and social achievement. They are a self confident and live by the motto "time is money."

A Middle Eastern Conflict

There is not one Arab-Israeli conflict but a wide variety of different confrontations that are connected to each other. The conflict with the Palestinians is a classical conflict of two national movements with each claiming the same territory as the other. The conflict between Israel and the Arab countries is another one and it includes national, geographical, political, cultural and religious aspects.[208] There are also bilateral conflicts between Israel and every single one of the Arab countries, even if they are not direct neighbors of Israel. These conflicts stem from the long history Islam and Judaism share in common and are also due to the geopolitical situation of the region. This international, supraregional conflict also arises because of differing claims to hegemony in the Middle East.[209]

The Six-Day War, 1967

In May 1967, Egypt expelled UN troops from the Sinai Peninsula and simultaneously imposed a blockade on Israeli ships in the Suez Canal. These actions sparked off another war. Jordan and Syria sent their armies to fight on the Egyptian side. Iraq and Saudi Arabia also deployed units. Not a single Palestinian fighter joined these forces because they had taken refuge in countries that did not trust them. Secondly, Palestinians were prohibited from raising an army of their own in these territories. After years of Egypt-initiated Palestinian Fedayeen attacks on Israel from their base in the Gaza Strip, the Six-Day War began.

Among other territories, Israel captured the rest of the Palestinian Mandate: i.e. the Gaza Strip from Egypt, the West Bank from Jordan and the Golan Heights from Syria. The war was over within six days. Shortly after Israel seized control of Jerusalem, it asserted its sovereignty over the entire city. The Palestinian residents of East Jerusalem were given permanent resident status in Israel. In one fell swoop, Israel controlled the entire former British Mandate of Palestine including the entire Sinai Peninsula. As a result, about 50,000 Palestinians escaped from the Jordan Valley into Jordan.

The War of 1967 was a big watershed. Israel conquered the West Bank from the Jordanian Legion within a few hours, without firing a single shot. Israel was praised in the West for scoring a spectacular victory in a war largely provoked by Egyptian and Syrian miscalculations, and partly by clumsy Soviet diplomacy. The Arab–Israeli War became an important arena for the Cold War.

After the War of 1967, the armies of Egypt, Jordan and Syria were completely defeated, especially the countries' air force. The West Bank, the Gaza Strip, the Golan Heights, and the Sinai Peninsula with all its Palestinian inhabitants came under Israeli control.

Opinions after the War

Eduard Said speaks about the rights of the Palestinians and he is correct to be outraged about the "non-existence" of Palestine,[210] but I doubt if he himself would have ever returned to the region. In his book *The Politics of Dispossession*, he mentions that the Palestinian problem did not arise until 1967 and was first considered by a vote at the United Nations General Assembly in 1969, after the territories came under Israeli occupation.[211] Nobody in the Arab world, not even the Palestinians themselves, tried to create an independent Palestinian state after 1948 because it would not have been possible under the totalitarian Arab regimes. Only Palestinians who were not refugees were the ones who kept living in the part of Palestine that became part of the Jewish state of Israel. "Israel was a device for holding Islam at bay. Zionism and Israel were associated with liberalism, freedom and democracy."[212]

Democracy in Israel, writes Hadawi, is a privilege only for the Jews—not for the Arab-Israelis.[213] Yet, the first time Palestinians started to talk about a country of their own was in an Israeli democracy, never under the Arab regimes before 1967. Of course, the Israeli democracy has many defects, but Israel is still the only country in the Middle East where one can stage a protest without being shot at.

One should not forget the fact that during the Six-Day War of 1967, Israel conquered territories in Egypt, Jordan and Syria, not territories of a Palestinian state because there never was a Palestinian state.

During my interviews with Arab-Israelis, many of them said that they do not want to be identified with the Palestinians in the Occupied Territories. They have rejected the idea of living in an independent Palestinian state on television and in newspaper interviews with Israeli media.[214] How bad can Israel thus be?

Demography after 1967

Before the Six-Day War the population of the West Bank numbered 840,000 people. 250,000 of them fled during the war. In Gaza the population numbered about 353,000 people, and nobody left the region. In the Golan Heights, around 7,000 remained and about 100,000 Syrian citizens escaped before the Israeli army invaded the region.

Since 1948, around 92,000 Palestinians have come back to the region either by infiltration—mostly from 1948 to the 1960s—or through family unifications permissible under Israeli law. About 100,000 Palestinians from the Occupied Territories have come to Israel as visitors after 1967 and have remained illegally. Others have immigrated illegally to the Negev, to Galilee, to Jerusalem and other places. All together, the estimated number of Palestinians who have come to Israel since 1948 is believed to be more than 300,000.[215]

After the War of 1967

The Arab-occupied Palestinian territories did not come under Israeli control until the Six-Day War of 1967. As a result, the Palestinians remembered that they had wanted an independent state. With the exception of the Palestinian Liberation Organization (PLO), all Palestinian national organizations were founded after 1967. A new Palestinian national movement started in the West Bank and Gaza. The reason for this was that the Occupied Territories not only came under Israeli control after the Six-Day War of 1967, but Palestinians also dared to express their wishes in words and actions. Now that the whole world was aware of their situation and willing to find a solution for the Middle East in general, and for the Palestinians in particular, they saw a chance to establish an independent state.

In addition, however, as much as Israeli mismanagement in the Occupied Territories is to be criticized, it is still the only democracy in the Middle East. This has meant that the Palestinians were able to start working on the project of an independent nation. They certainly were not able to realize these goals under various Arab regimes, which interned most of the Palestinians in refugee camps and never allowed them to lead a normal life, to obtain citizenship,[216] education, proper housing, etc.

The war was in fact not about Palestine but about leverage, benefits and gains of land for each Arab country involved in the conflict. The Arab countries neighboring Israel had their pride injured after losing the war against Israel, and wanted to rectify this insult.

New national feelings surfaced in Palestine. As a result, a few new national organizations such as Fatah were founded with the help of Arab countries in about 1968.[217]

Scoring a swift victory in the Six-Day War made the Israeli government overly confident. It is obvious that it did not consider the consequences of having over one and a half million Arabs under its control.[218] As history shows, Israel made a big mistake that actually created the "Palestinian problem."

We know now that the Six-Day War was a pyrrhic victory. Not only did it change Israel's position in the region, but it also altered the country's self-image. The few who protested against the occupation and the settlements on political or demographic grounds were ignored.

Settlement Ideology

"Right-wing and religious fundamentalists endowed the Six-Day War with a metaphysical, pseudo-messianic aura, and the settlements they initiated were at first financed mostly by nongovernmental agencies such as the United Jewish Appeal, the Jewish Agency, and the National Jewish Fund, often on land confiscated for 'security' purposes from its Palestinian owners,"[219] writes Amos Elon. He described the post-1967 occupation as "perhaps the least successful attempt at colonialism."[220]

The War of 1967 was a watershed in the history of the Middle East. Very soon after the Israeli victory, Israel started to build Jewish settlements in the newly Occupied Territories. Most of them were built by religious Jews from the United States. The most influential

American rabbis sent their followers to the territories to colonize an entire country given to the Jews by God. They themselves, however, never went to live there.

In Israel, a never-ending cycle of oppressive occupation and ensuing martial law started. More than 150 settlements and cities containing more than half a million Jews had populated the West Bank by 2012.[221] It seems as if this process will never stop. The Israeli government uses every trick to continue building more and more apartments and houses in the occupied West Bank and to harass the Palestinians even during so-called "peace talks."

Opinions

"We are speaking of a time (1967), thirty years ago, before the Palestinians were radicalized by an increasingly humiliating occupation regime and by a large-scale expropriation of Palestinian land for the exclusive use of Israeli settlers. Neither Hamas nor Hezbollah existed yet, and the PLO was not recognized internationally. Hamas was backed by Israel as a counterweight to the PLO. The failure to reach an agreement seems all the more tragic, since at that time there were still relatively few settlers; now they are one of the strongest political lobbies in Israel. At their core is a group of fanatic nationalists and religious fundamentalists who believe they know exactly what God and Abraham said to each other in the Bronze Age. On both sides now, extremists have the upper hand… There is no trust between Israel and Palestine. The extremists of Greater Israel and the extremists of Greater Palestine mutually veto all progress,"[222] writes Amos Elon.

The Six-Day War of 1967 left the professional classes and the intelligentsia very dissatisfied, and the continuing state of emergency provided powerful arguments for postponing fundamental reforms.[223]

"A world consensus condemned the occupation, and dozens of illegal Israeli settlements whose rationale was an anachronistic biblical argument were established. ... The world public could see Israeli soldiers patrolling Arab villages and towns, occasionally killing, usually beating Arabs... As a result, more and more Palestinians considered the PLO their only political representative,"[224] writes Said.

On December 5, 2013, Mathew Cassel, an American Jewish *Aljazeera* journalist, interviewed many Americans, Jews and non-Jews, and was told that "the Jewish lobby considers it its duty to support Israel in any matter and any resistance towards a Palestinian state. They do not concern themselves with the human rights of the Palestinians." Professor John Mearsheimer of the University of Chicago says that the Jewish lobby is one of the most powerful groups in the United States, that every American President since George Bush has been in favor of a Palestine state and against more settlements, but they had to backtrack because of the Jewish lobby. Many members of parliament on both sides are supporting this lobby.

It is unbelievable that these Jews talk about the rights of Israel and forget the rights of the Palestinians on purpose. Why can't they behave like real human beings and Jews who have always considered humanity as one of the pillars of Judaism? They don't understand that the survival for the Jewish state of Israel is predicated on an independent Palestinian state.

The Birth of Palestine

The actual birth of an independent Palestinian national movement in parts of former Palestine occurred after the War of 1967 when over one and a half million Palestinian Arabs came under Israeli occupation. The national movement laid the cornerstone for a state of Palestine, even if it was not yet recognized by the United Nations.

A strong demand for a political identity was voiced in 1967, after years of oppression by the former occupiers, the Arab states. Freedom was something the Palestinians were not supposed to strive for, let alone demand. Benedict argues that as the Palestinian generations of the 1960s and 1970s realized that in addition to Israel, Egypt and Jordan were also enemies, non-resistance against Israel seemed a viable option. Many Palestinians worked in Israel although they were often terrorized and blamed for being Israeli collaborators. Many new factions emerged in the late 1960s, approximately 20 to 25 different groups, and cooperated with Lebanese, Syrian and Iranian supporters.[225]

Yasser Arafat's most important goal was to create a Palestinian nation and a Palestinian state. He was only able to realize his first goal. Until Arafat came to Palestine, the Palestinians were ruled by outside powers within the Arab countries such as the Arab League. Some of the Arab Israelis and those living in the West Bank and in Gaza belonged to low-income social groups, because many of them were *Falahin*, farmers. They never had an opportunity to find refuge elsewhere and—in contrast to the Palestinian elite—did not have money or contacts abroad.[226]

Nobody Wants the Territories

In the aftermath of the War of 1967, when peace treaties with Egypt and Jordan were signed in 1979 and in 1984, neither of these states wanted to take the Occupied Territories back. King Hussein (1953-1999), the son of King Abdullah, was afraid to give shelter to more Palestinians in his country since he had experienced many difficulties with them since 1948. The Egyptians wanted the Sinai Peninsula back, but not the Gaza Strip with its enormous concentration of Palestinians (which totaled about 350,000 people; within the 45 years to follow, the population reached an estimated two million people). Israel entered into direct talks about a return to/withdrawal from the West Bank with King Hussein of Jordan, which was part of Jordan from 1922 to 1967, but in the end both countries refused to take the Territories back. In September 1970, after Palestinian-staged riots in Jordan, the Jordanian army crushed the Palestinian resistance in what went down in history as "Black September." The PLO was subsequently banished from Jordan.[227]

It was not until 1974 that the Arab countries decided at the Rabat Conference that the West Bank would not become part of Jordan and that the PLO was "the only legitimate representative of the Palestinian people."[228] The same happened with the Gaza Strip. After the peace treaty with Egypt was signed and Israel retreated from the Sinai Peninsula, the Egyptian government did not want to take Gaza back. They would not listen to any argument in favor thereof. They refused for a good reason—Gaza was named a "hornets' nest" which nobody wanted to administer. It subsequently passed into the hands of Israel as an Occupied Territory.

In fact, Israel was left with the Palestinian problem because Egypt and Jordan refused to take these territories back. Historically speaking, it sounds almost cynical if we say that the Israelis are the only ones who can give the Palestinians a state of their own, in the interest of both countries. Unfortunately, Israel has missed the opportunity time and again.

The Pre-War Period, 1972

It should not be forgotten that Israel had achieved unquestioned military superiority by 1972. Thousands of Soviet advisers had been dismissed from Egypt after the defeat of 1967. The American government considered Russian influence in the Middle East on the decline, and it no longer was of immediate Israeli interest to make territorial concessions. The Israelis were convinced that the Arabs would never dare to go to war again because they could not hope to defeat Israel. Israel's good fortune and an economic boom aided by cheap (Palestinian) labor gave rise to much complacency and perhaps even arrogance. Israel concluded that it had no urgent reason to change the status quo and that it should wait for the Arabs to start negotiations without preconditions.

In the 1970s, Palestinians assassinated many Israeli civilians by launching suicide bombs and hijacking airplanes. In Munich, Palestinian terrorists attacked the Israeli delegation to the Olympic games and killed all Israeli athletes. The Palestinian terrorists of Munich went to Libya after the attack and were invited to stay there. This situation ended with the Yom Kippur War of 1973.

The Yom Kippur War, 1973

The Yom Kippur War was the longest of the Arab-Israeli wars. The Arabs caught Israel by surprise, and in the first three days it looked like Israel would lose the war. The Egyptian army crossed the Suez Canal and marched to the Sinai Peninsula. At the same time, the Syrian army marched to the Golan Heights. Israel managed to push back both armies. Within a week, Israeli troops reached Damascus and after crossing the Canal, were on their way to Cairo. Many military experts say that after being humiliated repeatedly by Israel, the success of these first days rebuilt Arab confidence and laid the grounds for peace talks between Egypt and Israel as well as Jordan and Israel.

"The Arab-Israeli War of 1973 brought some benefits for Palestinians on an international level ... A great increase in wealth and influence of the Arab oil states was reflected in a new awareness of the Palestinian struggle for self-determination,"[229] writes Mansfield.

During that period, the Arabs put a general boycott on Israel in order to isolate it and gridlock its economy.

The most important reason for this change of heart—especially in the Western world—was that the oil-producing countries (mostly Arab), threatened an oil boycott, which could have paralyzed industrial development worldwide, given rise to unemployment and sparked off a world economic crisis with unforeseeable consequences.

The war lasted for almost three weeks, with many political scientists considering this development the basis for the peace with Egypt in 1979 and with Jordan in 1984.

Israel in Lebanon, 1982

In 1982, the Palestine Liberation Organization (PLO) was based in Southern Lebanon and fired *katyusha* rockets into northern Israel. Israel entered Lebanon and invaded all of southern Lebanon in order to chase the PLO out of the region. This attempt ended successfully, but soon Hezbollah replaced the PLO, becoming an armed organization with the goal of expelling the Israelis and eliminating the state of Israel.

Yitzhak Rabin (1922-1995)

Yitzhak Rabin was the biggest beacon of hope Israel had since its establishment. He was the first Israeli leader to speak to a Palestinian leader—Yasser Arafat—eye to eye. Rabin's political credo was to fight against the terrorists and hold peace talks with the moderates. After several Palestinian terrorist attacks in Israel, he closed the border of 1967 to Palestinian workers. About 120,000 Palestinians lost their jobs in Israel and their families had to suffer because of a handful of murderers. It was an attempt to separate Israel socially and economically from the Occupied Territories in order to stop terrorist attacks on Israeli civilians.[230]

When Arafat settled in Gaza in 1993, several right-wing Israeli leaders went berserk. They attacked Arabs and destroyed Arab property in the old city of Jerusalem in order to prevent Arafat from entering the region. In spite of all of this, in September of 1995,

Arafat and Rabin signed an interim Palestinian-Israeli agreement—Oslo 2— about the West Bank and Gaza. The American president Bill Clinton, the Egyptian president Hosni Mubarak, and King Hussein of Jordan attended the ceremony. In November of the same year, during the biggest peace rally ever to take place in Tel Aviv, more than 150,000 Israelis demonstrated in solidarity with Rabin's peace politics. Dreams of a peaceful resolution were short-lived. In November 1995, during a peaceful demonstration, a young religious Israeli educated by fanatical religious Jews assassinated Yitzhak Rabin. These "teachers" had incited the young man to kill Rabin in the name of God. At the funeral, more than 80 leaders from around the world[231] paid their last respects to Rabin. Rabin had become the symbol of hope to most Israelis. He represented a solution to the Palestinian-Israeli conflict and advocated for a life of peace. When he was murdered in 1995, it was by parricide.[232]

"A few weeks after the assassination of Yitzhak Rabin at a peace rally in Tel Aviv, the country is still swept by shame, shock, pain, guilt, remorse, and mutual accusation. In the latest polls, 74 percent of Israelis feel they must stand up in favor of the peace settlement Rabin advocated for. The police investigation of the self-confessed murderer and his alleged accomplices brought out in the open the seedy underworld of ruthless Israeli terrorists, informally allied with fairly prominent religious leaders, rabbis, mystics, cabalists, and other salvation-mongers,"[233] writes Amos Elon.

Yasser Arafat (1929-2004)

As one of the results of the Oslo Peace Talks, Yasser Arafat was given permission to enter Palestine in 1993. He lived in Gaza until his death in 2004. Arafat headed the PLO from 1969 to 2004 and was elected Palestinian president in 1989.

In 1983, Arafat was deported from Syria to Lebanon, from where he was later evacuated to Tunis. He was a subtle politician. In 1985, without declaring his purpose, he was ready to recognize Israel and to abandon the armed struggle in return for an independent Palestinian state, although it was risky to convince the Palestinian majority of such a difficult venture.

In November 1973, Arafat addressed the United Nations General Assembly for the first time. After the War of 1973, "the key Arab states, notably Egypt, wanted peace. For the Arabs, the prospect of recovering Palestine was as remote as ever."[234] The Palestinian Convention of 1964 was changed on Arafat's behest in 1988. Henceforth, the clause about the destruction of Israel was deleted.

In 1988, the King of Jordan declared that "he was abandoning all responsibilities for the West Bank." It was the starting point for the PLO to declare the establishment of an independent Palestinian state with Arafat as its president. The PLO was willing to recognize Israel and to renounce "all forms of terrorism." Arafat was advocating a "two-state solution." The Israeli leaders doubted the intentions of the Palestinians, but the United States, to the dismay of Israel, was willing to begin a dialogue with the PLO. This act changed the situation of the Palestinians, but in the end their hopes were not fulfilled. Israel's Prime Minister Shamir was convinced that time was on Israel's side and kept the status quo; his opponents, on the other hand, were convinced that the demographic clock was ticking against Israel.

"Yasser Arafat, 'Mister Palestine' himself, signed the Oslo Paper in 1993. He might have made mistakes along his way, but he remained a person belonging to his world. ... His idea of peace was rejected by his own people as a capitulation."[235] Arafat could have upheld the idea of a Greater Palestine, but he was realistic enough to see that this would not be possible. He therefore made use of his second best chance and signed a treaty with the Israeli government of Yitzak Rabin in 1993. Very few Palestinian intellectuals stood by his side. Many of his political and ideological companions of 30 years abandoned him, among them the poet Mahmud Darwish, the scholars Edward Said and Hisham Shar'abi. They preferred to maintain their hatred towards Israel and call for a return of Palestinian refugees from the Arab world to Palestine.[236]

It must be said that the above-mentioned intellectuals never lived in Palestine and under no circumstances considered living there. If you live outside the region, it is easy to oppose a compromise. Only the ones who experience an occupation and are subject to discrimination on a daily basis are entitled to decide about their country's destiny.

Arafat was the one leader who actually invented a Palestinian identity, and as such he will go down in the history of Palestine and the Middle East. He did not reach the goal of a Palestinian state during his lifetime.

Political Movements and Palestinian Organizations

Overview

The withdrawal of Israel from Gaza in 2005 did not bring peace nor did it ease the Israeli-Palestinian relationship. Quite the opposite happened. Hamas completely separated Gaza from the West Bank, where Fatah had won the elections. Two different ideologies were based on different political premises and entities. "Islamic activism was the first home-grown ideology in the Arab world. It gained currency in the 1980s and 1990s because it thrived in the one non-governmental institution no Arab dares to ban: the mosque."[237] Wrote Fuad Ajami.

The Palestine Liberation Organizations (PLO) was established in Cairo in 1964. Its goal was the liberation of Palestine through armed struggle, but it never was able to accomplish its goal. The original PLO Charter stated that a Palestinian state should be established on the territory of the former British Mandate prior to 1948 and proclaimed a "national duty ... to purge the Zionist presence from Palestine."[238]

King Hussein was against the organization and later forbade any of its activities in Jordan. The Syrian government felt they were outmaneuvered during the conference of 1965 and turned to Fatah, a Palestinian organization set up after the War of 1956. This organization was prepared to take action against Israel from within Syria. The idea was to provoke a war against Israel. "the sooner the better." This warmongering led to the Six Day War of 1967.[239] "The War of 1956, the Sinai War between Israel and Egypt, left the Palestinians on both sides of the border in peace because they were not the issue."[240]

In 1958, Albert Hourani wrote that the biggest problem of the Palestinians was "that of a whole community that wishes to go on living as a community. The continuing struggle for the liberation of their colonized land is their vision of a common fate."[241]

It was not until the Arabic Summit Conference took place in Rabat, Morocco, in 1974 that the Palestine Liberation Organization was recognized as the only legitimate representative of the Palestinian people. At this conference, it was also decided that the West Bank, which was annexed by Jordan before the war, would not be given back to Jordan but to the Palestinians, with the purpose of creating an independent Palestinian state. A month later, Arafat was invited to speak at the United Nations General Assembly, which decided to recognize "the right of the Palestinian people for a national self definition."[242] King

Hussein wanted to annex the West Bank and Israel would have also liked this solution, but by now it was too late. King Hussein subsequently ordered the closing of PLO's Amman offices.

Fatah[243]

Founded in 1965,[244] Fatah, the largest Palestinian organization, seems to have led to an increase in Palestinian militant organizations. Fatah's ideology is based on a Nasserite Sunni Islamic cultural ethos. Its first leader was Yasser Arafat (1929-2004).“[245]

As Fatah ruled the West Bank, it would have been the ideal counterpart for peace talks with Israel, but its government was too weak to change the status quo. As Israel keeps building more and more settlements, even the most moderate among Palestinian leaders feel provoked.

Israel will not start talks until the Palestinians recognize its right to exist as a Jewish state. This is understandable, but it may be too strong a demand as long as Israel does not stop the settlements and the illegal annexation of Palestinian land. Israel therefore has to change its policies and in turn recognize the right of the Palestinians to have a state of their own. Exposed to Iranian influence and economic pressures, Syrian leaders Hafez al-Assad and subsequently his son Bashar supported and encouraged Hamas, which was headquartered in Damascus. They also supported the Shiite Hezbollah and Amal organizations headquartered in Lebanon, and Islamic Jihad, which has branches in Palestine, Lebanon, Egypt, and Yemen. These organizations are active against Israel, the United States and moderate Arabic countries such as Egypt and Jordan.

Hamas[246]

Hamas is a Palestinian Sunni Islamic organization based in Gaza. It was established in 1987 as an ideological Islamic movement, a sub-branch of the Muslim Brotherhood. Hamas won the first Palestinian elections in Gaza in 2006. It has a military and a social welfare sub-organization. The intifadas of 1997 and 2000 were initiated by Hamas.

Elected in Gaza in 2006, Hamas severely weakened Fatah in Gaza through savagery and bloodshed. On the one hand, Hamas has connections to Iran, Syria, and the Muslim Brotherhood. On the other hand, it depends on Israel—with whom it has refused to talk—for its supply of water, electricity, pharmaceuticals and food products, as well as permission to move in and out of Gaza. The border between Gaza and Egypt is *de facto* closed because the Egyptian government fears that Hamas is a prolonged arm of the Iranian-influenced Muslim Brotherhood and will infiltrate Egypt to undermine the legitimacy of the government and disrupt the stability of the country.[247]

While Fatah obtained the majority vote in the West Bank in 2006, Hamas won in Gaza. Each wanted to become the sole representative of the Palestinian people. Hamas put enormous pressure on Fatah members in Gaza, humiliating, arresting, and killing hundreds of them.

The Palestinian Liberation Organization started to flourish after the Arab defeat in the Six-Day War of 1967, when the territories came under Israeli occupation. Within two years, Fatah and other organizations recruited thousands of volunteers. The PLO was founded as early as 1964, but the occupation gave it a new view on its duties and work. The PLO became the umbrella organization of all Palestinian movements and therefore the representative of the Palestinian people in the Pan-Arab League. Arafat became president of the PLO in 1969.

Hamas and Islamic Jihad

Receiving support from Iran, the Hamas and Islamic Jihad factions were against a peace settlement with Israel in opposition to Fatah and its leader Arafat. Both groups drafted an agenda of terror and violence against Israeli locations and civilians. Prime Minister Rabin banned 400 Hamas activists to Lebanon. He knew that peace talks could not resume as long as Israel suffered civilian casualties on a daily basis.

Iran successfully thwarted Israeli-Palestinian peace efforts by supporting Hamas in its policy against the peace talks and Hezbollah attacks from Syria and Lebanon. This cast a heavy shadow on diplomatic efforts to bring peace closer.[248]

Hezbollah[249]

Hezbollah was founded by Muslim clerics in Lebanon and has been funded by Iran since the Israeli invasion of Lebanon in 1982. During the Lebanese Civil War of the early 1980s, it primarily offered resistance to the Israeli occupation.
Hezbollah is a Shiite Islamic organization based in Lebanon. Hezbollah leaders have made numerous statements calling for the destruction of the state of Israel, or—in their words—"the Zionist entity." A number of Shia groups have slowly been assimilated into the organization, such as Islamic Jihad, the Organization of the Oppressed on Earth, and the Revolutionary Justice Organization. Their only goal is to eliminate the state of Israel.

Characteristics of Political Movements in Palestine

Fatah, Hamas and other smaller movements are national organizations deeply rooted in particular traditions. They are not Jihadist, even when they refer to Jihad— suicide and martyrdom—in their fights. They allow women to carry out suicide attacks, and their fight is against national injustice.
By contrast, Jihad is a transnational, fundamentalist movement for a religious Islamic idea rooted in the wider Islamic world. The Jihadists are Sunni Muslims that fight against Shia Muslims, Israel, and the West in an equal manner.
There are many organizations that use various names, but belong to the same ideology of Jihad and are connected with each other. They see themselves as a moral movement that is designed to fight for Islam. There are no women in their ranks. They are mostly against everything that is not Islamic according to their own interpretation and understanding of the world. Salafi Muslims and Al-Qaida are Jihadist movements.[250]

Intifada

Young Palestinians started the first Intifada in 1987 because they wanted to draw attention to the hopelessness of their situation. The Palestine economy was structured entirely along colonial lines and the Arab states appeared to have lost interest in the Palestinian cause. Two years after the Palestinians came under Israeli occupation, some 50,000 were arrested, 7,000 wounded and 500 killed. More than half of casualties were under the age of eighteen. People who were suspected of collaborating with Israel were killed on a daily basis.[251] Due to Palestinian agitation, the political landscape in Israel changed from left to right and then back again until it firmly stayed on the right.[252]

The Intifada of 1987

The first—spontaneous—Intifada of 1987 interrupted the economic symbiosis between Israel and the people living on the West Bank and in Gaza.[253] It broke out not because of a national uprising but because of poverty, inhuman living conditions in the refugee camps, hatred towards the occupiers and above all the two decades of humiliation of the Palestinian people.

Another reason for this uprising was that Palestinians felt neglected and let down by the Arab world. The first Intifada, which lasted from 1987 to 1993, gave rise to Hamas in Gaza.[254] In 1988, the national liberation movements declared an independent state of Palestine.

The Intifada of 2000

In 2000, the Second Intifada began. During the second half of the 1990s, Iraq had invaded Kuwait. Some of the only people to stand behind Saddam Hussein were the Palestinians. They were dancing in the streets and celebrating his triumph. By celebrating the Iraqi president as a hero, they damaged their reputation on an international level.

In 2004, Israel staged a one-sided withdrawal from the Gaza strip, but maintained control of the air space and the coast.

This Intifada lasted until 2006, when Hamas won the elections in Gaza and released its official legislative program. The document clearly signaled that Hamas would be willing to recognize Israel in a national referendum. This was a major shift away from their 1988 charter, which had called for Israel and the Palestinian Territories to be converted into an Islamic Palestinian state. A few months later, the group sent a letter to the American president George Bush stating that it did not mind "having a Palestinian state within the 1967 borders" and asking for direct negotiations. Both Fatah and Hamas were never able to agree on who would rule Palestine. Since then, the West Bank has been ruled by Fatah, the Gaza Strip by Hamas.

Places of Refuge

The Arab Countries

When we look at the refugee problem around the world, we realize that during the twentieth century hundreds of thousands of people became refugees, especially in Europe, yet nobody is talking about these people's right of return, because it is objectively and practically not possible.

As mentioned before, between 1948 and 1967, most Palestinians lived under occupation in Egypt, Syria, Lebanon and Jordan. These countries never considered either a Palestinian state or the integration of the Palestinian refugees in their territories. Starting in 1948, the Palestinians were refugees in their own homeland, which was not their country, and remained this way until they came under Israeli occupation in 1967. The ones who went to other Arab countries suffered the same fate. They were crowded into refugee camps with no rights, no citizenship, no education and—for lack of passports and affiliations—hardly a chance to go abroad. To this day, the UN organization UNRWA has tried to cover their basic needs.

Palestinians have been kept hostage in the Arab countries for all of these years first and foremost because their Arab brothers do not want these "troublemakers" in their countries. Secondly, their presence gives these countries a good argument against Israel. As long as they are not integrated and retain refugee status, a possible return to their homeland can be used to pressure Israel.

"The Arabs, in their army barracks and the academies, in the capital cities of the Arab world—Beirut, Baghdad, Damask, Cairo—built their own 'dream palaces,' and intellectual buildings of secular nationalism and modernism," writes Ajami in his critical book about the Middle East, Arabs and Jews and the odyssey of a whole generation. "Arabs suffered a broken heart after their nationalism collapsed and left them severely frustrated."[255]

Refuge Outside the Middle East

The other refugees[256]—those who went to the United States, Europe or elsewhere—integrated well in their host countries and, with the exception of the first Palestine-born generation, mostly do not consider themselves refugees anymore. It is interesting to analyze the lives of those who immigrated to countries outside of the Middle East. I have met and spoken with many Palestinians in Europe and the United States. They are not interested in returning to the land of their ancestors. They have integrated, have benefited from a good education and built their homes. The generations that were born there are only Palestinian by origin, and mostly do not identify with Palestine.

According to the Palestinian Central Bureau of Statistics, 11.2 million Palestinians lived around the world in 2011:

2.6 million in the West Bank

1.6 million in Gaza

1.37 million in Israel (within the borders established in 1967)

5 million in Arab countries

636,000 in countries outside the Middle East

44 percent of the Palestinians in the Occupied Territories and the Arab world are refugees.[257]

The Right to Return

"The Palestinians have repeatedly insisted on their right to return, their desire for self-determination, and their stubborn opposition to Zionism as it has affected them."[258] The fact is that none of the Palestinians living out of Palestine, either in the Arab world or outside the Middle East, ever considered coming back to Palestine as long as they were under Arab occupation, like on the West Bank or in Gaza from 1948 to 1967. It is actually not clear why they did not return. Were the host countries against it? If yes, why? If no, why not?"

"It is useless for a Palestinian Arab to deny the conviction and intensity of genuine passion, just as it is useless to imagine that Israeli Jews would be likely ever to want to return to their places of origin."[259] Would Europe consider taking the Jews back if they would have wanted to return? "The fact is that Palestinians and the Israeli Jews are now fully implicated in each others' lives and political destinies (...) which is a subject not easily approached in rational discussions, but certainly should be now and in the foreseeable future." [260] The earlier both nations realize this fact, the sooner they will start working on a future together.

Even the Palestinian people know that it is not impossible for all Palestinians to return to their original homeland. In this context, I would like to draw a comparison between the European Jews that were murdered, expelled and displaced by the Nazis, and had to leave behind their property. For various reasons, only very few went back to their countries of origin. But let us assume that the Israelis would have liked to return. By now it would be more than 3 million people who would go to Germany, Austria, Poland, Hungary, etc. Does anybody believe that these European countries would welcome them with their children, grandchildren and partners? The European solution was to pay restitution. This is what should be done with the Palestinians as well as with the Jews from the Arab countries, who also had to leave barehanded. Restitution for everybody is the only way forward.

Another question arises in this regard: Why do Palestinians outside the Arab world not want to return? As I mentioned before, I asked some Palestinians who live in the United States and Europe and their answer always is, "This [new] country is my home. I was born and educated here. I belong to this country. I'm (American, French etc.) of Palestinian origin but I have very little interest in going to a place I did not come from, and to which I don't belong. The Palestinian question only applies to my grandparents, who came from Palestine."

In 2012, the UN General Assembly resolution Nr. 67/19 stipulated that the state of Palestine would replace the PLO as a UN observer.

Said writes that the Palestinians are "a divided, oppressed community with no territorial sovereignty."[261] He blames the "Zionist" for causing the Palestinian problems, but forgets to mention that, firstly, the Palestinians never had their own state to begin with; secondly, that the idea of going to Israel and make it a homeland for the Jews is a Zionist idea, but very few Jews followed the call; thirdly, that most Jews came to Israel because they had to fear for their lives in Europe after 1933 and no country welcomed them on its territory. With the creation of the state of Israel, the problems of European Jews were pushed onto the Palestinians and in turn most of them were pushed out of the region.

To this day, some of the Palestinian refugees in the Occupied Territories and most Palestinians in the Arab countries still live in refugee camps and the question of how their situation should be resolved remains one of the burning issues in the Israeli-Palestinian conflict.

Palestinian Education

"The Palestinians ... are a political 'football' for the Arab states. ... They seem to have the highest educational attainment of any other national (Muslim) group there,"[262] writes Said. Is it possible that Palestinians have achieved this high level of education because they have to abide by Israeli educational law, or because out of the nine universities in the West Bank, eight were built after 1967? When I studied Arabic at the University of Vienna, my colleagues and I were all surprised about the fact that the Palestinians are the only Arab nation with almost no illiteracy.

Palestinians were oppressed by their Arab brothers under whose rule they lived from 1948 to 1967. They lived mostly in refugee camps and were not allowed to work or study (except partly in Jordan). The same never held true for Palestinians in Israel. Yes, they were not equal citizens, but they still had rights and lived in their own homes, villages and cities. They have had access to higher education and health services and they attend Israeli universities. Even if they are not equal, they are more equal in Israel than in Arab countries. "The opportunities for education inside Israel have not been the same for Arab-Israelis as for Jewish Israelis,"[263] writes Said. Compared with the Palestinians living in Arab countries, however, Israeli Palestinians have benefited from many educational opportunities. Arab Israelis are free to attend high schools and universities in Israel.[264]

Before 1948, a wide network had been laid for Arab secular education in Palestine, but in 1948 most teachers and intellectuals left the region. Israel saw the restitution of Arab education as its moral responsibility. Later, Arab teachers, educated in Israel, took charge of education. "There are thousands of Arab Israeli students in every Israeli university, many Arabic authors and journalists who publish literature and articles in Hebrew and Arabic, pro and contra Israel. So, why are they dissatisfied? The stronger a subgroup becomes, the louder are its demands. It was natural for Arab youth in Israel to follow the trends prevailing in the neighboring countries. Since freedom of speech was granted under Israeli rule after 1967, full use was made out of it. ... While the majority of the Arab masses still adhere to their traditional ways, Arab Israelis have benefited from the Western civilization of Israel despite their status as second-class citizens,"[265] writes Goitein.

The educational system on both sides unfortunately includes negative narratives of the other as the enemy. Children on both sides are growing up with hate and suspicion towards the other side.

Since the Occupied Territories came under Israeli legislation in 1967, all children have had to attend schools until the age of fifteen. Therefore, almost every Palestinian can read and write, which is not the case in the rest of the Arab world, where between 20 and 60 percent of the people are still illiterate and hence easier to rule.

List of Universities and High Schools in the Occupied Territories

- Birzeit University was the only Palestinian university that existed before 1967.

In the West Bank

- Arab American University
- Al-Quds Open University
- Al-Quds University
- An-Najah National University
- Bethlehem Bible College
- Bethlehem University
- Birzeit University
- Edward Said National Conservatory of Music
- Hebron University
- Ibrahimieh College
- Khodori Institute, Tulkarm
- Palestine Polytechnic University

Al Ahlia University of Palestine

In the Gaza Strip

- University of Palestine
- Al-Aqsa University
- University College of Applied Sciences
- Al-Azhar University - Gaza
- Al-Quds Open University

- Islamic University of Gaza
- Universal Studies Academy
- Palestine Technical College

The above mentioned educational and research institutions are not the only ones in the territories.[266]

Israelis and Arabs

"Everybody in the Middle East loves to hate the 'others.' The Arab countries resist a democratic state of Palestine. ... If war is too serious a matter to leave in the hands of the armies, peace is too important a matter to leave in the hands of governments,"[267] writes El-Mahdi. As the case of the Egyptian-Israeli peace shows, it is better to have a cold peace than a war. This is also the opinion of many Egyptian intellectuals whom I interviewed in Cairo and Alexandria in 2009. All of them have expressed regret that it is not a really warm peace.

One of the biggest issues in the Israeli-Palestinian question is that most authors have a clear stance: against Israel and in favor of Palestine, or against Palestine and in favor of Israel. Having just another opinion does not do either regime a favor. It is either "us" or "the others." What we do is correct; what the others do is wrong. The national narratives are similar. They are full of hatred for and suspicion of the other,[268]writes El-Mahdi, and I completely agree.

What Do People in the Middle East Want

People on both sides want to go about their business, earn a good living, have a nice house and give their children good educational opportunities. Most people are completely distanced from religious radicals on both sides, who have never worked a day in their life nor served their country in any other way.[269] Jewish radicals are against Israel's retreat from the Occupied Territories. These radicals send their young people to occupy the territories by building settlements and thereby lead Israeli soldiers into conflicts—often against the soldiers' will. Arab radicals send their young people to die in the Holy War against Zionism.[270] Young people on both sides do this in the name of God, Elohim or Allah, and religious justice.

One of the most dangerous aspects of the Palestinian-Israeli conflict is the religious element. It is actually not a religious struggle between Judaism and Islam.

"The demographic demon is more alive than ever, although the right-wing policy tries to bury him."[271] Between 1967 and 1987, under the Israeli regime, living standards as well as fertility rates rose considerably in the West Bank and Gaza.[272]

Religion as Handicap

Religious radicals on both sides were unable to see it this way, let alone the fact that those on the Jewish side never took part in fights or wars themselves because they are the only group in Israel that are not obliged to serve in the military. They never saw the necessity of giving up one square inch of Israeli territory for the sake of peace. On the Islamic side, religious groups have sent their followers to do the dirty jobs; on the Jewish side, the Israeli army has resolved the situation for the settlers. Israeli soldiers have had to protect the settlers even when they themselves are against the settlements. The Oslo Accords of 1993 showed that a solution to the Israeli-Palestinian problem was possible for the first time in 44 years. These accords brought an ironical symmetry in the criticism levied against Arafat on the Palestinian side and against Rabin on the Israeli side. They were both condemned as traitors who were involved in an unacceptable compromise.[273]

El-Mahdi had the following to say about the settlements: "It is not justifiable that 400 settlers in Hebron are protected by 2000 Israeli soldiers, who put 30,000 Palestinian citizens under a curfew."[274]

The Religious Aspect

"The [Arab] idea of the elimination of Israel is equal to the [Israeli] idea of wanting all of Eretz Israel for themselves; these ideas complement each other and give each other legitimacy," writes El-Mahdi. He is also aware of the fact that the religious groups that block progress towards peace on both sides are getting stronger and more powerful. He wonders why religious groups have become very important contenders in this conflict, especially after the Six-Day War of 1967.[275]

Arabs, Israelis, and Palestinians

PLO spokesperson Abd er-Rahman declared on June 12, 1988: "Our biggest problem is not the bullets of the enemy [Israel], but the Arab countries—especially Jordan, Syria and Lebanon—that try to prevent a Palestinian state with all their might because they fear that it might have a negative effect on their countries," said PLO spokesperson Abd er-Rahman on June 12, 1988.[276]

The Arab-Israeli wars always ended in ceasefire treaties, never in peace agreements.

The Palestinians have always been used as pawns in the greedy expansion plans of their Arab neighbors, who after 65 years cannot accept the fact that Israel is an integral part of the Middle East and will never vanish. Many still consider Israel an intruder that should be removed. Even though most Arabs know this is not possible and will never happen because "Palestine had also become a bone of contention in inter-Arab politics" and: "[the Israeli-Palestinian conflict] involved both rivalries between progressive and conservative forces..."[277]

Israelis and Palestinians

Until the Territories came under Israeli occupation after the War of 1967, there had always been a territory called Palestine, but never a state. When a Jewish state was established on

May 15, 1948, most Arabs who used to live in Palestine left or were expelled from Israel. They went to live in other countries in the Middle East or outside of the region. They consider themselves Palestinians. By contrast, the Arabs that stayed in Israel refer to themselves as Arab-Israeli.

Even scholars such as Edward Said, who was of Palestinian origin and strongly criticized Israel, wrote that the questions of a Palestinian people as well as a Palestinian state were non-existent until the Territories came under Israeli occupation after 1967. He dedicated his book *The Politics of Dispossession* (New York, 1995) to the Palestinian question and to what he calls "the record of hostility between Jews and Arabs ... between Palestinians and the rest of mankind." But he also says that he is horrified "about the terror … in Palestinian men and women who were driven to do such things [as launching suicide bombs]."[278] And later, "The task then became to convert Palestine into a Jewish state ... on the systematic denial of a substantial native Arab presence in Palestine."[279] He does not consider the original partition of 1947, in which the Palestinians would have received about 45 percent of the land. Their Arab neighbors were opposed to such a solution, and nobody even asked the Palestinians if they wanted to accept the partition or not. It must also be said that the Palestinians were not organized, and did not have institutions that would have been able to administer a new country. The Palestinians lost their entire homeland instead of losing only a part of it because their Arab brothers had to wage war against Israel and thereby lost a country that did not belong to them. Palestine has not existed since February of 1949, and Israel and the Arab countries have ruled the region that used to be Palestine. The Arab countries are to blame for this—not the Palestinians or the Israelis.

Palestine

Said writes that with the exception of the Palestinians, no other group in the Arab world ever proposed a "secular democratic state with a Muslim, Christian, and Jewish population..."[280] We should consider this as maybe one of the biggest problems with a concrete Palestinian state. Since no democratic state has so far been established in the Arab world, it seems that the leaders of the Arab countries are afraid of this form of statehood. As Palestinians have lived under Israeli occupation for more than five decades, they have a sense of what democracy means—and it can be assumed that a Palestinian state will be a democracy, even if it will be different from the kind of democracy practiced in the West. Neither Israel nor the Western World can teach Arabs or Palestinians democracy because it is a question of integrity, understanding and interpretation and it differs from country to country.

Arab countries may not want to see the emergence of the first Arab democracy because it might ignite the democratic flame in other Arab countries and therefore could change the political map in the Middle East. "Who can be sure now that Egypt, Lebanon, Jordan and Syria really want the same Palestinian self-determination that the Palestinians want?" doubts Said, adding that the Arab countries have done nothing for the Palestinians.[281]

In all polls held in Gaza and the West Bank during the 1990s, the majority of Palestinians said that they wanted "democracy and free elections."

The Middle East

"The Middle East has more heavy arms and is more mobilized for war than any other region in the world,"[282] writes Said. Neither Israelis nor Palestinians realize that they have always been puppets in the hands of outside powers and that this part of the world has been important to too many big powers for its fate to be left to its inhabitants.

After World War II, the Cold War between the Soviet Union and the United States affected the Middle East as well. The Russians had Egypt and Syria as allies. The United States had Israel, Jordan and Lebanon on its side. The superpowers engaged in a competition for allies and satellites and more influence on the ground; later the Palestinians were misled by their brothers who had a lot of oil revenues—and hence economic power worldwide—such as Iraq and Saudi Arabia.

The Curse of the Status Quo

"From the beginning, Israel only reacted instead of taking the initiative to create a better Middle East for all nations that live there."[283] Palestinians wrongly assumed that time was on their side. For a long time, the Israeli government preferred a political and geographical status quo. It was simply convinced that this status quo would stay that way forever. The religious Jews of Israel and the entire world were against returning any land to the Palestinians for religious reasons (because God had promised this land to the Jews). Many American religious Jews built settlements in the West Bank because their rabbis had told them to populate the Holy Land given to the Jews by God. The Israeli government has supported the settlers and provided aid on the ground, which ran counter to any productive peace initiative and prolonged the status quo.

The dangerous job of protecting the settlements is left to native Israeli soldiers, no matter if they agree or disagree with the government's settlement policies. These soldiers often have to serve in the Occupied Territories against their conscience and conviction.

Though many Arab countries donate money to Palestine, they have never invested in infrastructure, education, or business. Their money goes towards training young people to become shahids (martyrs) and commit acts of terror against Israel or other countries, or towards weapons and ammunition for the fight against Israel. Families of assassins receive money for their sons and daughters who kill Israeli civilians in suicide attacks.

Many Jews abroad have invested in Israel or in illegal settlements in the West Bank, and the settlers deliberately provoke Palestinian inhabitants, whose land is diminishing right before their eyes every day. For example, olive plantations are disappearing because Jews expropriate them with no consideration or respect for the original owners.

Israel and the Arab World

"An objection to normalization with Israel is the most popular measure to incite hatred against Israel and fuel fears. ... Israel wants normal relationships with the Arab world, not only through a signed peace treaty but also through economic and cultural exchange,"[284] writes Avidar. It is true that Israel wants peace and tranquility, but it is not prepared to pay the price and give up some of its illusions. Israel it totally isolated in the region, both in terms of its culture and of its philosophy, and this scares other Arab countries. They fear that Israel will become a leading power in Middle Eastern culture and economic matters. "Our ignorance brings with it a 'dialogue of the deaf,'" says Avidar. He also describes the Arab world as a huge mosaic rather than a monolith. The same also holds true for the Islamic religion. One of the most important rules in the Middle East is that "each country is to itself" as far as its interests are concerned. Israel has always been arrogant and supercilious towards its neighbors. This attitude has negatively affected its relationships.[285] Still, Israelis must be aware of the fact that its Arab neighbors cherish the concepts of honor and pride and many of them have low self-confidence. This, in turn, means that Arabs are very easily insulted. Israelis on the other hand are very self-confident and sure of themselves. As these two cultures and traditions are very different, misunderstandings occur.

One of the big differences between Israel and its Arab neighbors is that the Arabs are traditionally educated to cherish collectivism, while Israelis are educated to be individualistic. The only way to communicate is to accept one another even without understanding.

Today, in spite of the animosity between Israelis and Palestinians during many years of conflict, Arabs remain very curious about Israel, which they consider a big power in politics, economics, the military and technology. Israel is mentioned very often in the Arab media. According to Hugi, there have been instances when Arab journalists have been excluded from the writers' association or arrested and incarcerated when they have dared to show their support of Israeli culture or politics.[286] It looks as if totalitarian regimes in the Arab world feel more threatened by Israeli culture and politics than by its military power.

In his book *After the Guns Fall Silent*, first published in London in 1976, Muhammad Sayyid describes a possible peaceful solution for Arabs and Israelis. He wonders what the Middle East will look like after a lasting peace is established. In the Arab world this subject is taboo among intellectuals as well as among the population at large. Peace agreements with Egypt (1979) and Jordan (1984) have shown that the situation of not having war is good for all, but otherwise nothing has changed. As long as no agreement exists on the Arab side to accept the state of Israel, Israel will never believe Arab countries really want to establish peace. An anxiety about Israel's technological superiority has always been a stumbling block. Arab countries fear that once a lasting peace is established, Israel will dominate the region economically.[287] In 1976 people were not allowed even to think this way in the Arab countries, let alone write about it, and therefore Muhammad Sayyid Ahmed was heavily criticized in the Arab world.

Dr. Abd el-Hamid Ansary, an accredited authority and publicist from Qatar, found some answers in an article published in the newspaper *Al-Bian* (based in the Arab Emirates): "Why does Israel always whine?" His answer to the question is very simple: Israel is a problem-solving culture based on self-criticism. Israelis correct their mistakes and learn from their failures, and never put the blame on others. Why is this attitude not prevalent in the 300 million people in the Arab world? Because then Arabs will have to realize that blaming others is self-deception.[288] The Arabs will never know why Israel wins wars: they remain defeated. Even though Dr. Abd el-Hamid Ansary's book was never officially reviewed, no Israeli could have explained it better.

Peace Talks

It is the longest peace process in world history.

Israeli-Palestinian peace talks are primarily concerned with ending the occupation and settlements, establishing a territory for peace, and compensating both Palestinian refugees and Jews from Arab countries.

The Peace Conferences of Madrid (1991) and Oslo (1994) [289] were hopeful steps in the right direction. A solution seemed to be within reach, yet they ended with only a few insignificant decisions. The most serious attempt on the part of the United States to promote a general settlement of the Arab-Israeli conflict, writes Shlaim, was the Madrid conference of October 1991. The biggest problem remains the Israeli settlement policy in the West Bank—especially the fact that many settlements have been built around Jerusalem and that Palestinian territory has been confiscated through the destruction of villages. Time and again in the name of security, Arab soil has been confiscated and homes have been destroyed. Shlaim's opinion is that the settlements have been established to undermine the peace process, which is based on the idea of "territory for peace," which does not seem to be a point of Israeli political interest[290]. Yitzhak Shamir's (1915-2012)[291] speech as Israeli prime minister was narrow minded and aggressive against the Arabs in general and the Palestinians in particular. He did not accept a PLO delegation as Palestine's official representative, although this organization was accredited as such on an international basis. Palestinians therefore participated as part of the Jordanian delegation. Although it was an affront toward the Palestinian delegation, the speech of the head of the Palestinian delegation (Dr. Haidar abd el-Shafi from Gaza) stood in absolute contrast to the Shamir's. "Our and your security and safety are conditional on each other."[292] It was an impressive and moderate speech, but it did not help start a constructive dialogue towards peace. In December 1991, the United States initiated the Washington meetings despite Israeli objection; the Israelis delegation did not appear. This move had an impact on Israeli society, however, which started to show more willingness to accept the idea of "territory for peace" than its government.

In 1993, the Oslo Conference on Israel and Palestine began. The talks culminated in the White House with Yitzhak Rabin, Yasser Arafat and Bill Clinton as a mediator. It was one of the strongest images of the twentieth century,[293] and it showed a diplomatic revolution in Israeli foreign politics because the country had realized that the problem could only be solved through peaceful negotiations. Within eight months, Rabin and Arafat managed to meet 14 times, all under the utmost secrecy. The Israeli government confirmed this fact unequivocally.[294]

Palestinian and Israeli fanatics tried to torpedo the talks.[295] The public in the Arab world—especially intellectuals—would not hear of any kind of talks with Israel. Syria, Iran, and Iraq; Hamas and Jihad;[296] and the Israeli settlement policy in the West Bank (in the name of Jewish claims to this land since biblical times), stood in the way of these and all other peace talks.

The settlement policy started right after the end of the Six-Day War in 1967, and has continued without interruption throughout both right-wing and left-wing Israeli governments. The settlements have sounded a death knell to the talks.[297] Both Arafat and Rabin tried to avoid open confrontation with their inner opposition. They tried to successfully conclude the Oslo meeting, an attempt at which they unfortunately failed.

With the assassination of Yitzhak Rabin in 1995 by a fanatic religious Jew, no other politician of his caliber could fill his shoes. A historical moment had passed and never returned.

"The peace treaty between Israel and the Palestinians had not yet been signed in Oslo in 1993 when a new battle began. The fear of Israeli military superiority was replaced by a 'horror' of the cultural hegemony of Israel,"[298] writes Ajami. "The secret peace between Israel and Egypt (1979) had put an end to all illusions embraced by the Palestinian intellectuals. ... The Oslo Peace (1993) was a different story. Yasser Arafat himself signed it. While the Palestinian Charter had once claimed that all of Palestine belonged to the Palestinian Muslims and Israel had no right to exist, Arafat and his Parliament changed this in 1996.[299]

Benyamin Netanyahu (*1949)

The newly elected Israeli government under Prime Minister Benyamin Netanyahu[300] came to power after a wave of terror swept through Israel. This wave of terror was instigated by Syria and Iran, countries that supported Hamas, Jihad and Hezbollah in order to stop the peace process. Unfortunately, they succeeded in their efforts. Palestinian terror scared the Israelis public into voting the right-wing Likud Party into power during the 1996 elections.[301] Netanyahu formed a cabinet with a coalition of three religious parties and two right wing parties. It was a religiously motivated, chauvinistic and ethnocentric government—and a declaration of war on the peace process.

With this new government, Netanyahu provided a new impetus for the restoration of Arab unity. The meeting in Cairo in the same year was the biggest since 1990, which was held during the Iraq invasion of Kuwait.[302] As a result, Arafat stopped any contact with Israel. Polls showed that about 75% of Israelis considered the establishment of an independent Palestinian state a must, and a logical result of the Oslo process.[303] Ehud Barak, then-minister of foreign affairs, said: "I believe that we must part with the Palestinians. We don't need apartheid in any form in this region, and not another Bosnia. With Netanyahu's politics we are likely to achieve both."[304] Netanyahu also spurred on the building of new settlements. Arab soil was confiscated, and the settlers were given free rein to abuse and mistreat the Palestinian population under Israeli occupation. Netanyahu put a wedge not only in the Palestinian population, but also in his own country and the entire Middle East.[305]

Ehud Barak (*1942)

In July 2000, the peace talks at Camp David took place for two weeks. Although there were no definitive results, Israeli Prime Minister Ehud Barak and the Palestinians made some progress in their bilateral talks. They addressed the rights of the Palestinian refugees, the evacuation of settlements, and Israel's release of Gaza as well as of 90 percent of the West Bank. The sovereignty of Jerusalem was also discussed.[306] Just like in the past, this agreement showed no results, as Israeli politics changed again after the new elections, during which Ariel Sharon emerged victorious. This new prime minister had started his political career by provoking the Palestinians and lighting the "Al-Akza intifada." He put every possible restriction on the Palestinians. His goal was to defeat, overpower and expel them.[307]

Ariel Sharon (1928-2014)

Ariel Sharon, Israeli prime minister from 2001 to 2005,[308] had to step down after a stroke. His first move as prime minister was to visit the Temple Mount, a sacred site for Jews and Muslims alike, with some 1,000 Israeli police officers. This act provoked the second Intifada of 2000. He was a commander in the Israeli army in 1948 and had took part in all Israeli wars ever since. After his retirement from the army, he became a member of the right-wing Likud party and made a historical move by stopping the Israeli presence in the Gaza Strip in 2005, while maintaining control of its coastline and airspace. All Israeli settlements in the Gaza Strip were also abandoned. This was viewed as a positive step towards a peace settlement by the Palestinian authorities as well as by Israel's left-wing parties. Benjamin Netanyahu, Ariel Sharon's biggest rival in the Likud Party, protested against this move. Unfortunately it did not bring the region any iota nearer to peace.

First Free Elections in the Territories in 2006

The first free elections of 2006 brought a victory for Hamas over Fatah in Gaza. The opposite happened in the West Bank. The Palestinian Authority tried to establish a coalition government between Fatah and Hamas, but the talks ceased after only three month. Fatah and Hamas could never come to terms. The result was that Hamas took full control of Gaza and tortured, deported, arrested, and killed many Fatah members.[309] A Hamas-led government has never recognized Israel's right to exist. A short time after the elections, Israel and the United States declared the Palestinian Authority of Gaza an anti-Israeli terrorist organization.

Israel started to boycott Gaza, yet the only way to get humanitarian aid to the region was through the passage between Gaza and Israel, as the border with Egypt had been closed hermetically. The Israeli government decided to leave the passage open, but restrict supplies to humanitarian aid such as drugs and food. Israel kept supplying Gaza with electricity and water and let hundreds of trucks pass in order to transport goods to the population of Gaza. This situation prevailed even during the Israeli bombardments in 2008 after Hamas had constantly bombarded Israel with missiles.[310] According to Avidar, the Hamas uprising in Gaza was a result of a one-sided withdrawal on the part of Israel.

Mutual Recognition

Most Arab countries as well some of the Palestinian leaders were against the creation of a Palestinian state, especially because it is based on an agreement with Israel, which entails a recognition of Israel. This was decided at the meeting of the Palestinian Board in July 1968, which was the highest Palestinian institution at the time and included almost all Palestinian national organizations.

Israel, by contrast, was the one country in the Middle East to recognize the Palestinian rights to the land by agreeing to the partition plan of 1947. The Arab countries rejected that plan, and never took into account the destiny of the Palestinians.

Arab leaders did not want to agree to the establishment of a Palestinian state, not least because they would have lost ground to Israel and would no longer have been able to argue that the destiny of the Palestinians was tied to Israeli oppression and the non-existence of a Palestinian state. People in the Arab world remain quiet because they only have one thing in common: they agree that Israel is their beloved common enemy. Most Arab countries are in agreement with each other on this and only on this. The Israeli threat and the wish to wipe Israel off the world map—although they know this will never happen—bind them together, or, as Ajami puts it: "The only glue for (…) Arab loyalty is hostility towards Israel."[311]

There is another reason why most Arab states are not interested in a Palestinian state: as the Palestinians have lived under Israeli law for over 45 years—which, despite all arguments to the contrary, is still a democracy, a form of government unknown in the Arab world—they might establish the first Arab democratic regime, as experienced by two to three generations of Palestinians under Israeli occupation. Arab leaders are in a panic because this will probably have a big impact on the entire Arab world. It might show that an Arab democracy is possible, and this is exactly what no Arab leader is interested in.

One of the reasons for the Arab countries to support the Palestinians with sophisticated weapons and ammunition instead of new schools, universities and hospitals is to keep them in their daily misery, fighting for basics like food and housing.

Support from Abroad

For Israel

Despite the Arab oil embargo and other embargos of the 1970s, it seems natural that the West—primarily the United States and Europe—are pro-Israel. The Western world understands the Israeli way of thinking and acting, the culture, which is based mainly on Western European values, better than they could ever understand the Arab mentality and priorities.

In spite of all criticism towards Israeli as regards the Palestinian question, one cannot ignore the fact that this society is built on social democratic European ideas based on humanism. Israel is a constitutional democracy with civil liberties, even if not all of its citizens are equal under the law and Arabs are often oppressed. The fact remains that almost all Israeli-Arabs claim time and again that they will never live in Palestine once it becomes a state.

The Israelis, including those who came from the Arab countries, dress and think like Europeans. Their culture is modern and high-tech.

Israel is the only reliable partner of the West in the Middle East, and a safe haven for the sixth float of the American navy in the Mediterranean Sea. Military treaties between governments are honored, even if the country changes direction politically. This is not always the case with treaties signed by Arab countries.

For Palestine

Palestinians mostly receive aid from Arab countries and Iran, although the United States and Europe also do their share to support them. It is unfortunate that rich Arab countries primarily support Palestinian guerilla fighters with arms and ammunition, mostly through illegal channels along the Sinai Peninsula, or by giving money to families whose sons or daughters commit suicide by bombing targets in Israel and in the Western World. About fifteen years ago, rumors were circulating that families of suicide bombers received about $20,000 for every child that "successfully" carried out a suicide attack. These rumors cannot be substantiated. Poorer countries such as Syria, Iran or Libya support Palestinian jihadists by training them in terrorist camps. These countries fuel Palestine's hatred towards Israel through military education. They teach them how to build bombs and design strategic ways to force the West and Israel to their knees.

Fear and Suspicion

Yitzhak Rabin was the first Israeli leader to sign an agreement with Yasser Arafat. Rabin became prime minister in 1992, and his declared goal was to establish peace between Israel and the Palestinians. He was committed to the motto "land for peace," yet he did not stop the building of settlements in the Golan Heights, around Jerusalem, and in the entire West Bank. These two facts are incongruent, but Rabin's actions were often contradictory. Rabin still represented a big hope for peace among Israelis despite their fear of the consequences. Similar feelings also prevailed among the Palestinians. Rabin's assassination in 1995 brought all talks to a standstill and crushed all hopes.

The mistrust between Palestinians and Israelis is one of the biggest obstacles to a peace agreement.

Many Palestinians gave up hope when they realized that even during peace talks the Israelis kept building more and more settlements in the West Bank. They mistrusted their leader Arafat, when he talked with Rabin while more settlements were being built—a total contradiction to the peace talks.

Israelis are afraid of bombs and suicide attacks on civilians, and they have a right to defend themselves by any means necessary.
Palestinians are mainly afraid of not being heard by the world, of being forgotten and left with their oppression. They commit acts of terror to raise awareness of their situation.
As long as these two peoples cannot live with each other, they might as well live separately and wait for new generations that might—and hopefully will—be able to live next each other without falling into a permanent paranoia.
Israel staged a one-sided withdrawal from Gaza to separate the two peoples and avoid more clashes, but this maneuver did not work.

Partnership

Many Israeli leaders claim that Fatah is not an adequate partner to engage in peace talks because Mahmud Abbas (*1935), who was elected head of the Fatah in 2006 in the West Bank, is too weak, and he does not dare make decisions that are essential for peace; headed by Ismail Haniyeh (*1963) since 2006, Hamas still does not recognize the state of Israel. Israeli leaders are also powerless because religious Jews wield a strong influence in parliament as four religious parties tip the balance of power.
Another fact is that a majority of Palestinians and Israelis (more than 50 percent, sometimes even 70 percent) want a "two-state solution"—not because it is ideal, but because it seems to be the only logical solution.

The Dreams, the Wishes

In 2000, the Camp David Talks took place. We do not have exact records of what was being said at these talks. When they came to an end, the Palestinian and Israeli participants told different stories and had different interpretations of what was being said. An official statement was not issued.
The dreams of both sides to obtain " all of Eretz Israel" or "all of Palestine"—i. e. the land from the Mediterranean Sea to the Jordan River—ended in frustration.

Two main approaches exist in the Israeli-Palestinian debate: one is a secular, rational approach; the other is a religious, irrational approach. The first one is usually performed on a political level, and includes rational arguments rooted in a changing political reality. The second one is based on religious axioms and tries to bend reality to religious faith. It is rooted in antiquated religious laws and traditions, and is subject to religious authority.

Religious sects in Palestine believe that all of Palestine belongs to them. Israeli sects are convinced that all of the God-given territory of Eretz-Israel belongs to them. Religious groups in Palestine claim that "the war will continue until the last piece of the Land of Palestine is rescued" (until it all becomes an Arab land). Religious fanatics in Israel say that "in the name of the divine promise, Israel will fight until Eretz-Israel will return to the Israeli /Jewish people—all of it, forever." Politics and history have shown that neither one of these diametrically opposed wishes can become a reality. Instead, a solution must take into account the socio-political history of the two peoples as well as security aspects.

The idea of two countries for two people came out of the recognition that in view of great differences in national, religious, cultural, economic and social agendas, as well as demographic developments, a one-state solution is an absolute illusion. As Palestinians have a much higher population growth, Israel would soon become another Arab country in a single state. The reality of the early 21st century is that a two-state solution is the only reasonable option.

Secure Borders

The question of security has always been a top priority for Israel. This was the case in 1948, and it is still the case after 1967. The assumption that the 1967 borders are easier to defend than those of 1948[312] can only be explained with the fact that those border are farther away from Israel's highly populated areas and can therefore be defended more easily. Both Israel and Palestine would be better off developing energy resources to create more infrastructure, and secure jobs, as well as developing culturally and socially instead of stockpiling more weapons. Both peoples should learn to respect each other in the name of humanity and to create a future for all children in the area. It would no longer be necessary to secure the borders. When over one million Palestinian tourists visit Israel and vice versa, the two countries' economies will boom. But the most important thing to work on is independence from the influence of other powers.

Borders are a political decision between two countries. As one can see when traveling through Europe, borders do not have to be barriers. They become less and less important when the threats are gone.

Common Borders:

A border is a fence, imagined or real. It signals separation and partition, two sides of one thing, closeness and proximity, joint possession, commonality, neighborhood, immediate vicinity and a conviction and condemnation to live side by side.

Said writes that he can empathize with Israel's fear of destruction after what Jews had to go through during the Holocaust and that he understands that security is a top priority for the country. However, according to Said, the Palestinians cannot be held hostage to that fear, "which is a disaster for them and for the Jews. ... Two things are certain: the Jews will remain; the Palestinians will also remain. ... The people of Palestine and Israel are tied together through their past and future."[313]

Terror

Major general Amos Gil'ad, head of the political security department of the Israeli Defense Forces, said at a conference in September of 2011: "We succeed at our 'war against terror' thanks to our security ties with the Palestinians and Abu Maa'sen's rejection of terror..." in the West Bank. Israel could not reach any agreement with Hamas in Gaza, however, and had to withdraw from this territory in 2005.[314]

According to Arieli , the Kassam Brigades—the military branch of Hamas—published the following figures in December 2011 relating to its military activities since its foundation:

11,000 rockets and mortar bombs were fired into Israel.
1,365 Israelis were killed.
6,411 were wounded.
1,117 attacks were carried out, 24 of which were kidnappings.
1,848 of Hamas fighters were killed.[315]

The Winners

Israelis who live in the West Bank receive about €20,000 each family from the Israeli government to buy a home. They also receive discounts on educational expenses and health care. Among other ideological and moral problems, the problem with these settlements is that their maintenance costs the state of Israel dozens of times more than the same houses within the green borders of 1948.
The price Israel pays for the settlements is out of proportion and a real burden to the state. It is increasing as more settlements are built.
I have listed some of the economic negatives of the occupation here. Overall, according to a report in the Israeli magazine *Globs* in May 2005, the cost for the occupation had amounted to at least 100 billion Israeli Shekel (US$35 billion).[316] Israeli society also incriminates itself from an ethical and moral viewpoint because of the occupation.

Israeli Society

Even if Israel succeeds in solving all security and economic problems, some central questions remain: does Israeli society want to rule another nation by denying it their civil rights? Is this how the Jewish community wants to educate its children? Is this the only way to exist and is it even worth the effort? Is the risk of withdrawal from the West Bank and having the Palestinians closer to Israel's urban centers bigger than the risk incurred through occupation? As I stated before, a majority of Israeli intellectuals foresaw this development as early as 1967, yet when they tried to warn the country, but nobody would listen to them. After all, Israel had just received a big boost of self-confidence through a military victory.

Israel has to escape from this stalemate by focusing on constructive efforts and being aware of the dangers that threaten all its achievements. Noam Chomsky puts it this way: "In general, each military success simply reconstituted the struggle at a higher level of bitterness and hostility (...) of military force and of potential danger to all concerned. From the Israeli point of view, this is a losing strategy. Israel can win every conflict but the last." Even if Israel were to draft the peace treaty itself, this treaty would not guarantee security. The result is that Israel is forced to be increasingly dependent on the United States. Arabs also follow a losing strategy. This will lead to continued destruction, to the strengthening of the reactionary and repressive forces from within, and to increasing dependency on the imperial powers from outside. That can only lead to an even bigger tragedy in the Middle East.[317]

Shimon Shamir, an Israeli historian and expert on Middle East Jewry writes, "Israel pays a high price for maintaining the occupation. The country loses the spirit from which it has derived its strength. It is doubtful whether Israel can again mobilize the same spirit of solidarity to resist threats of extermination as in its founding days."[318]

Comparison

"The Jews were not ousted by their European governments, but left out of their own free will because they either disagreed with, or did not wish to live under changed political circumstances. There is no law or policy in all of these countries to prevent their return if they wish to do so. The Palestinians ... are still eager to return,"[319] writes Hadawi. I wonder how ignorant he is that he does not understand that the Jews did not leave Europe out of their own free will, and that most countries around the world did not want to reintegrate Jewish refugees after World War II. Jews could not stay in Europe because genocide occurred during the war and they could not return to their countries of origin after the war because their torturers continued to live in these countries. The foundation of the state of Israel was the best thing that could have happened to European countries that had put Jews into displaced persons camps and treated them as outcasts. In addition, these countries neither wanted Jews to return and reclaim what was stolen from them nor did they want them to stay as a living reminder of the perpetrators' deeds.

And what about Jews from the Arab countries and their right to return to their countries of origin? Nobody has even taken this option into serious consideration after November 1947 and the creation of the state of Israel in 1948.

Returning the Occupied Territories

A return of the occupied territories is a fallacy because one principal question arises: to whom should they be returned? There was never a Palestinian state, and until 1948 there was not even a Palestinian nation. First, Israel conquered the territories from Egypt, Jordan and Syria—countries that had invaded Israel in 1948 when it was still a United Nations protectorate. Secondly, after the war of 1967, neither Egypt nor Jordan made any efforts to regain control of these territories. On the contrary, Egypt and Jordan did not want the territories.

Out of all countries in the world, Israel is the only one than can help facilitate the foundation of a Palestinian state. For generations, the Palestinian people have had natural and legal rights *de jure* to their territory. The Palestinians are the natural successors to the Egyptians, who did not want to reclaim the Gaza Strip when the peace treaty between Israel and Egypt was signed, and Jordan, which passed on its rights to the West Bank to the Palestinians in 1988. [320]

The above-mentioned countries, which in fact invaded the territories in 1948, were never asked to return it to the Palestinians.

Palestinians started to fight for their rights because that Israel is a non-Islamic democracy where resistance is permitted. In the Arab countries, by contrast, they would have had a harder time resisting the regimes.

"Normal Relationships"

"Normal relationships" between the Arab countries and Israel never existed.[321] Instead, everyday life in the region has been marked by a total Arab boycott of Israel in the 1970s, border collisions, violence and a constant arms race spurred on by the superpowers as well as by rich Arab countries—some of which are not interested in a solution to the "Palestinian problem."

The Zionists' biggest achievement was the creation of the state of Israel as a home for all Jews, which became necessary and had a moral justification after the Holocaust. The biggest failure of Israel is that it has not succeeded in ending its conflict with the Arabs—especially the confrontation between two national movements, the Israeli and the Palestinian. However, one should not overlook the fact that the creation of the state of Israel was based on an injustice committed towards the Palestinians or forget their subsequent suffering.[322] This injustice is irreversible given the present realities.

Press and Literature in the Middle East

Israeli Press

The Israeli press is the press of a democratic country in a state of war. Articles on military issues are censored. Major newspapers include *Maariv*, *Yediot-Aharonot*, and *Jerusalem Post*. *Haaretz* is the best source of information, however, because it voices criticism of Israeli politics, the behavior of the army in the territories, the occupation, the settlements and many other problems and injustices. Its journalists cover the problematic position of Israeli-Arabs, the occupation and settlements at least four to six times a week. It reports about the state of affairs and gives its readers a well-rounded picture of region.

Press in the Occupied Territories

Several Palestinian newspapers and magazines are voicing criticism of Israeli politics. They can do so because the Occupied Territories are located in the democratic state of Israel.

There are many Palestinian writers and journalists who write partly for the Palestine press—newspapers and magazines published in the Occupied Territories—and partly for the Israeli press, especially *Haaretz*. They publish their books both in Hebrew and in Arabic.

Unfortunately, self-criticism hardly surfaces on the Palestinian side. Not one Palestinian intellectual has pointed out the social errors of Palestinian society. They keep blaming others—i.e. Israel, for all that's wrong with Palestine. It's not as if critical writers do not exist. They are often just afraid they may risk their lives or be damned by their own people.

Israeli Courts

"UNICEF Report of 2013: Israeli Defense Forces are torturing Palestinian children who were arrested for throwing stones. The report says that children on both sides are being injured and killed, but overall more Palestinian children. Israeli soldiers testify that the way the children are being treated has a humiliating, arbitrary character. The Israeli Ministry of Foreign Affairs reports that it has already reacted to the accusations," the Reuters news agency wrote after a report appeared in *Haaretz* on June 23, 2013.

The Israeli lawyer Felicia Langer, who often defends Palestinian prisoners, states: "The military courts impose thousands of years of imprisonment on Palestinians in the Occupied Territories without any possibility of appeal." She claims to have seen marks of torture on the bodies of her clients. "Amnesty International therefore repeated its request for an independent inquiry into all aspects of this problem," she was quoted as saying in Hadawi's book. She adds, "The Israelis added refinements such as torture, collective punishment, expulsion and deportation, destruction of property and confiscation of Arab lands."[323] Even if all of this is true, the Palestinian prisoners still can rely on an advocate and a defending counsel.

Olive trees are being chopped down to make room for new settlements, without consideration of the moral and environmental value of the trees, which were often planted by the great-grandfathers of Palestinian families. It looks like this is being done on purpose, to show the Palestinians who is in charge.

Ethics and Sovereignty

Religious antagonism towards everybody non-Jewish runs very deep in Israel. Since this attitude is not based on logic or rational arguments, it can hardly be discussed. Secular antagonism is easier to handle because one is open to understanding logical arguments and facts.

Israel's New Historians were the first ones to analyze the conflict between Israel, the Arab countries and the Palestinians from a scholarly point of view by using documents that were released for public view in Israeli archives in 1988, after forty years of being kept secret. Yet the New Historians were not the first ones to write about the conflict. As early as the 1950s and 1960s, the Israeli intelligentsia—mostly the intellectuals and journalists—wrote about the double morality and the ethical problems that arise in a society that distinguishes between Jews and Arabs. At this very early stage, they warned about the changes and the impact this attitude could have on Israeli society. After 1967, these same people wrote about the occupation and the settlements, again condemning them as immoral, yet very few people listened to them—definitely not Israeli politicians and decision-makers. These authors took up a quixotic fight against windmills. Even after the first enthusiasm of the victory had waned, Israeli society was not ready to accept what they had to say.

The Israeli elite—writers and journalists—does raise its voice against the occupation and the settlements that started as early as the late 1940s. They first wrote about the discrimination against the Israeli-Arabs, and after 1967 about all other aspects of the occupation. They warned that human rights and equality—supposedly pillars of Zionism—were being violated, and yet they were mostly labeled as leftist ideologists. The large majority of the Israeli society willingly broke with national narratives even though it did so with a broken heart. In 1988, the New Historians started to publish their critical books.

When the Israeli national narrative and the perception of Zionism that Israelis had learned in schools and in the Army since 1948 changed, many questions no longer were taboo, even though it was not convenient to admit some Israeli wrongdoing. The research is restricted because a new freeze has been imposed on Israeli archives. If we talk about archives, however, it must be said that Israel's Arab neighbors as well as the Palestinian Authority do not have any archives at all, or they deny having them.

Interviews

Marwan Barghouti (*1959) is one of the first Palestinian pioneers and a very important supporter of the peace process. He is a well-known activist for the Palestinian cause. Many Israelis put high hopes on him, and think that he will be the person who will lead Palestine to peace.

Marwan Barghouti has served a jail sentence in Israel since 2003. "You must announce that the occupation is over and that Israel is leaving the territories ... [You must announce] a total withdrawal and the dismantling of the settlements and that you recognize an independent, sovereign Palestinian state with its capital in East Jerusalem ... Then everything will change. It will be possible to solve the refugee problem as well, believe me. I mean it ... but since the assassination of Rabin there hasn't been a peace process," he said in an interview with Ben Caspit of the newspaper *Ma'ariv* on November 9, 2001.

Ami Ayalon (*1945) was head of *shin bet*—the Israeli secret service—until 2000. "A two-state solution is the only path to true peace and security. ... There are more Palestinian terrorists today than a year ago, and there will be even more tomorrow! We are beating them, but why are they gaining strength? The Israelis were provided with a one-sided version: 'We were generous and they refused'. This is ridiculous. (...) Our state has a reason to exist only when it furnishes a homeland for the Jewish people and is a democracy; according to those two perspectives, time is against us! Demographically, it works for the Palestinians, and politically, in favor of Hamas and the settlers. In order to fight Hamas it is necessary to evacuate the settlements whose close proximity to the Palestinians fuels the hatred. It will either be a bi-national state, in which case it will no longer be a Jewish state—or remain a Jewish state—in which case it will no longer be a democracy. A complete disengagement from the Palestinian territories is urgently needed. And when [the Palestinians declare and independent] state, Israel should be the first to recognize it," he said in in interview with *Le Monde* on December 23, 2001.

Opinions

Yoram Kaniuk (1930-2013), Israeli writer (*The Last Jew*, 1948). Kaniuk was an Israeli patriot and one of the pillars of Israeli culture. He lamented the loss of humanism in Israel, one of the cornerstones of Zionist ideology, which Jews should not forget. He wanted the country in which he believed and for which he risked his life to remain secular and democratic. He believed that Israel should grant equal rights to all of its citizens. "Israel is not the country Zionists had dreamed of and fought for," Meged writes in his editorial in *Haaretz* on June 10, 2013. "Kaniuk was Israel's 'Baron Munchhausen.' He realized … the catastrophe occurring on both the Israeli and the Palestinian sides starting in 1948. He was always the antithesis to all the things we grew up with, which were false and brazen lies and which he could not accept a long time before it became part of the Israeli narrative. He was desperate about the occupation and the settlements and about the way Israel treated the Israeli-Arabs; towards the end of his life he obtained the recognition he was due as Israel's conscience," Eyal Meged continued in *Haaretz* on June 16, 2013.

The Israeli author **David Grossman** (*1954) wrote in his book *Present Absentees* in 1992: "One does not have to be a political or psychological genius in order to understand that there will be a bitter price to pay for the powerless situation of the Palestinians in Israel; a price for the insults and discrimination; a price for [Israel's] superiority … in the Occupied Territories; but above all, Israel will have to pay for its ability to ignore their suffering, the personal and the collective one, for the selective blindness …—the bill will be presented. ... With our haste, we are sometimes ignorant and often brutal or indifferent. In order to stop it we need only one tool—a 'wise heart.'"

A. B. Yehoshua (*1936) writes in his book *Between Right and Tight*: "Zionism succeeded because of the distress of the Jewish nation; and because of help it received from objective reality; the fear was deep in the people that once peace comes, the 'Jewish battles' (among themselves) about the religious question would start. ... We must strive to change our self-definition to strengthen nationhood and weaken religion. ... The Jewish orthodoxy is not able to change and does not want to change. ...)A dialogue can only happen outside religion." Both Arabs and Jews have historical rights to all of Eretz-Israel/Palestine. Therefore, the only solution is to divide the country between both nations. It is true that the Jews lived in other countries for many years and never tried to return to Israel; history gave the Jews a moral right to create the state of Israel. The same right should be granted to the Palestinians."[324]

In 1974, **Professor Harcabi** (1921-1994) published a small booklet titled *The Palestinian Convention and its Significance*, in which he tried to explain the Palestinian question to an Israeli public.

"The Palestinians, although they had a common language and culture, always felt they were aliens in the other Arab countries. Many did not want to improve their living conditions in the refugee camps because they did not want to admit to its permanence. They always dreamed of returning home to Palestine. We Israelis should recognize the fact that the Palestinians have an affinity to this country and we should not be surprised or shocked about it. They still do not have a territory, but they are a nation. Jews were in this situation for thousands of years and yet remained a nation. Palestinian refugees were never welcome in the Arab countries, which did not keep their promise to create a Palestinian state as long as they could keep the places they conquered in 1948. The Palestinians were only a sideshow that did not matter to them."

Haaretz: Israeli Newspaper

Articles and Essays

One of the best sources of information on Israeli politics and society is the Israeli newspaper *Haaretz*. Experts consider it the foremost newspaper in the Middle East because it allows thinkers from the entire political spectrum—Israelis, Arabs and international journalists—to present their opinions uncensored. As an acknowledgment of its courage, a few quotes of articles published in 2012 and 2013.

"Israel is increasingly turning into a religious and ethnocentric community, with no tolerance for any critics of right-wing ideas. Israel is nowadays viewed as a brutal country that lives in a constant state of anxiety and terror fueled by its own government. Israel considers every critic an antisemite.

Whatever looks like it is good thing for the Palestinians is viewed as a threat to Israel. Every foreign observer or journalist is considered an enemy (because everybody supposedly is against Israel). The Israeli prime minister adds to this confusion, but it cannot exist forever; it will explode one day, but until that time, Benjamin Netanyahu will keep up his resistance against Arabs, Palestinians, Israeli demonstrators, the left, the center, *Haaretz*, The *New York Times*, Europe, Asia, Africa, and Barack Obama. We have never been in a better position," Doron Rosenblum, senior correspondent, noted in an opinion piece in *Haaretz* on April 25, 2012.

The Battle for the Narrative

"There are claims that Palestinian leaders and intellectuals ran away from their homeland [in 1948], and shortly thereafter all those who could join them fled. They left their people without guidance. These claims also say that the Palestinians were told they should escape the region because they would be coming back to their houses and villages soon. Arabs states encouraged these escapees, but some Jews made efforts to stop them (research by Roni Gabai for his PhD thesis published in Perth, Australia in 1959). Dr. Moshe Ma'oz said in an interview, "The dosage was different (at the time), then it was stuck to the national narrative we were told in schools and in the army." Dr. Uri Stendhal, who worked with *Ma'oz* says that Ben Gurion did not know exactly what was going on. We cannot verify his claim because a total freeze has been imposed on Israeli archives. These archives house most of the documents that the New Historians used in the late 1980s about the expulsion and deportation of Palestinians in 1948 and 1949, the 'Nakhbah' and other events, Shai Hezkani wrote in *Haaretz* on May 17, 2013.

What is the historical direction of the state of Israel?

"What is the historical direction of the state of Israel? Its beginning was promising.
The Zionist project is a success story, if not a real miracle. The question at hand is if this project has an expiration date. The occupation and the settlement policy terminate this project. This subject means the defeat of Zionism, because as long as this policy is carried

out, Zionism cannot be implemented. Religious Zionism is responsible for the occupation and the settlements, which are the big political winners in the 'Israeli project.' A small, determined minority in Israeli society succeeds in imposing its will and values on a confused, silent and paralyzed majority (Unfortunately, all Israeli governments since 1967 have agreed to the settlement policy.) Their victory will be the end of Zionism. Even if they do not participate in a coalition government, they show everybody else who the real boss in Israeli politics is. Unfortunately, we Israelis don't have an Abraham Lincoln or a Martin Luther King to talk about what 'freedom' means," Uri Misgav wrote in *Haaretz* on June 1, 2013.

Conquest? Who? What? Where?

"A mechanism of denial is used to avoid the shame, anxiety, guilt and pain that are associated with any immoral action. A denial of facts is an admission of an unsolved problem that needs treatment. We have been in this state for 46 years. We deny one of the central facts of our national existence—the conquest. (...) When we deny it, it does not exist.

Israel invented something that is unprecedented—an eternal conquest. If Israel had annexed the Occupied Territories, it would have ben forced to grant the occupied population civil rights. As occupied territory, Israel can rule without granting the population any civil, civic or human rights.

Conquests destroy and corrupt the character of a society. The entire country is in violation of international laws on a daily basis. Only when we confess to the impossible situation, we can change it," Uri Avneri wrote in *Haaretz* on June 8, 2013.

A Jewish and a More Jewish State

"The legal system of Israel laid the groundwork for the two main ideologies of the state:

1. Israel's Jewish identity emphasizes the rights of the Jews to return to their country. It also posits the use of the Hebrew language, the affinity to Jewish heritage, and to religious festivals and holidays.

2. Israel's democratic identity was analyzed and established by the Israeli court in recognition of the principle of sovereignty, human rights, separation of power, and the rule of law.

Over the last few years, it has become more and more difficult to bring these two ideologies into harmony. Israel has accepted the rule of Judaism, or to be more precise—God. The messianic nationalistic Judaism that rabbis and politicians practice today is neither the Judaism of our fathers, nor of the ones who formulated Israel's Proclamation of Independence and the country's legal system. Chauvinistic extremism is tainting the original consensus of all layers of Israeli society.

This is the result of education and of a distorted, narrow interpretation of the concept of Judaism. Israel is approaching the status of a religious society.

And what about democracy? It is very quiet nowadays. Humanism and pluralism have taken a backseat to peculiar laws and a proposed homogenous way of thinking.

Racism towards Israeli-Arabs has been officially denounced, but this is not enough. Anti-racism should be one of the pillars of Israeli education," Itamar Kremer wrote in *Haaretz* on June 13, 2013.

"The Occupation Destroys Society, the Army and the Justice System."

Knesset member Shelach attacked the settlements and declared that the occupation destroyed the Israeli army, the media and Israeli society as a whole. "The settlements are the biggest obstacle that stands in the way of an arrangement between Israel and the Palestinians and this roadblock is getting bigger and bigger as time passes. Israel is becoming more and more like apartheid South Africa and its political standing is constantly deteriorating. The Israeli system of justice is based on a double morality—one for the Israelis, another one for the Palestinians. A political consensus is of utmost interest. We have to understand who we are by starting to clean up the system in which we live," Ofer Shelach said at the conference of the Arab Initiative at Hebrew University in Jerusalem in an interview with Jonathan Liss published in *Haaretz* on June 13, 2013.

Islamic movement

"It looks like the Islamic movement is one of the worst things to happen in Arab society in Israel. The same is happening with the Jewish society in Israel, however: religions groups in Israel are becoming more and more fundamentalist, thus preventing the creation of a secular national identity, which reigns supreme over all religions.
Religious indoctrination in general, and indoctrinations by monotheistic religions in particular, can be identified as 'advanced hatred.' The Israeli government should prohibit the foundation of religious parties by law. This law would not prevent anybody from practicing their religious beliefs, but it might stop religious incitement by racist religious agents, whatever their religion may be. Nothing good comes from religion," Salman M'salha wrote in an opinion piece in *Haaretz* on June 14, 2013

The Return of the Discrimination Law

"A legal bill for service to the country was approved by the members of the Committee on Legislation on June 15, 2013. If enacted, this bill will seriously question Israel's status as a democracy. Discriminatory practices, for example of Israeli-Arabs who by law do not serve in the Israeli army, will receive official approval. The country will have a right to favor those who served in the army in matters such as housing, employment, public services, higher education and more.
This law is a direct affront to the dignity of human rights. Israel's attorney general addressed the prime minister of the last Knesset because of legal difficulties. It is humiliating that the Minister voted in favor of the bill. If Israel wants to be seen as a democratic state, this bill should be thrown out," Amir Fux wrote in an opinion piece in *Haaretz* on June 17, 2013. Fux is a member of the Israeli Institute for Democracy.

Betrayal of our roots?

"The fact that we were integrated in a civic society and we do not live in a camp is seen by some Palestinians as a betrayal of our roots, and we have felt guilty about it. ... The idea of a return is an attempt to run away from the hostility and enmity of the world. If the Palestinians demand the right to return, it is only because they live in places that are hostile to them; and let's say the truth, the Arab countries are not especially friendly to the Palestinians," El-Youssef, a Palestinian writer who lives in a refugee camp in Lebanon, wrote in an article titled "Reflections About Having a Life in Civic Lebanese Society Outside of the Camp" in *Haaretz* on June 17, 2013.

I'm ashamed to be an Israeli

"I'm ashamed to be an Israeli because of the official political direction the country is taking. Instead of congratulating the Iranian voters, Israel is the only country in the world suspicious of the elections in Iran that brought in a moderate president. The Israeli cabbage heads are anxious that the country will no longer fear [Iran]; that it will become impossible to convince the Israeli public that Israel's situation is hopeless ... because of the Iranian nuclear development. The perverted, twisted priority of this government is the occupation and stealing of Arab land in the West Bank. They are afraid that more and more Israelis will understand that there is and must be another alternative. I'm sure that the moderates can win not only in Teheran, but also in Jerusalem. When will the moderates win in Israel?" Uri Misgav wrote in his blog for *Haaretz* on June 17, 2013.

The Settlement Myth

"As a result of big changes on the ground in the West Bank, especially with the settlements, the solution of 'two states for two people' is increasingly pushed to the side, but most Israelis are indifferent towards the settlements and prefer to leave the Occupied

Territories within the framework of a total Israeli-Palestinian agreement. The settlements are supported with billions of Shekels a year by the Israeli government (and religious groups outside of Israel). Without this help, they don't have a chance to survive. There is no infrastructure, and more than two-thirds of the inhabitants work within the green border. The settlements have no future, neither economically nor politically. Their residents live on money Israel needs for its own territory. Once a government stops supporting the settlements financially, they will cease to exist and not one soldier needs to intervene," Raphael Inbar, founder and director general of the Molad Center for Renewed Democracy, wrote in *Haaretz* on June 19, 2013.

Israeli scroll of independence

"Megilat-ha'Atzmaut, the Israeli scroll of independence, is screaming in pain, shock and shame about how Israelis behave towards Palestinians and Palestinian holy sites. My country, eliminate this craziness that has befallen you!" Haim Gury, one of the leading Israeli authors, wrote in an opinion piece in *Haaretz* on June 22, 2013.

Intellectuals criticize the Israeli government

"Intellectuals criticize the Israeli government for illegitimately occupying the territories, condemning it for its particular kind of ethnic chauvinism. There is no other country in the world that defines itself by its ethnic, religious or national pureness. Germany or France are countries for 'all of their citizens, regardless of their background.' There is no place for Israel's ideology in our age of mass migration. Would anybody in Israel support a country like this? Is its character legitimate in your opinion?" senior correspondent Gideon Levy wrote in *Haaretz* on June 23, 2013.

Right-wing politicians in Israel

"An official document shows that right-wing politicians in the Israeli government claim that only 1.5 million Palestinians live in the West Bank. This is a result of research conducted by the American Team for Demography, which serves the interests of the government by demonstrating that the 'demographic devil' is not a real threat to Israel. According to a document of the Israeli administration, 2.6 million Palestinians live in the West Bank. This document also says that since 2000 the population has increased by 29 percent. These numbers were verified in the 2007 census, which was carried out under Norwegian surveillance, the IDF, the United Nations and the Israeli Secret Service and most demographers in Israel. Adding the Israelis and the Palestinians that live between the Jordan River and the Mediterranean Sea, there are 49 percent Jewish-Israelis and 51 percent Muslim-Israelis. These numbers include the West Bank, Gaza and Israeli-Arabs. This means that the annexation of the West Bank will create a bi-national state," senior correspondent Nir Hasson wrote in the news section of *Haaretz* on June 30, 2013.

The political situation in Israel

"The political situation in Israel is a confession of failure. The state of Israel should be ashamed. The Jewish Home Party is headed by the xenophobic racist Rabbi Eliyaho, who often agitates against Israeli-Arab students in Safed and prohibits the sale of apartments to them in this city. Israel would have cut its diplomatic relationships with any European country that selects a religious leader and that speaks about Jews in the same manner as this Rabbi speaks about non-Jews in Israel. We just have to look at the apartheid regime in the Occupied Territories, the persecution and imprisonment of African refugees and the victimization of other groups to know that 'something is rotten in the state of Israel,'" Itamar Hendelman Smith wrote in an opinion piece in *Haaretz* on July 12, 2013.

A State of Jews, not of Israelis

"Israel has changed from an asylum for persecuted people into an exclusive, militant and racialized country. In any Western country, religion is a private decision. Currently, there are four religious parties in Israel. Religious values should be based on human rights and the universality of human existence. Only in that way can a society maintain humanist values and an equality of all its members regardless of gender, religion or race. Israel sees itself is a developed democratic society, but it is not interested in these values when a citizen is not Jewish.

In Israel, life is influenced by the Jewish religion as in no other country in the Western world, a world Israel is trying to belong to. Religious rules are forced upon the non-religious society, which is about 80 percent of the Jewish population of the country. Religious oppression is part of every day life, and the majority lets it happen.

On the Israeli identity card or passport, a citizen's nationality is not defined as Israeli, but Jewish (or other), which runs counter to Zionist ideas and ideals.

One is forced to eat kosher in most restaurants. There are no supermarkets that sell non-kosher products because religious groups are threatening non-kosher supermarket chains with boycotts. People are forced to have religious marriages. There is no public transportation on Shabbat, which means that the poor cannot enjoy the day because they cannot afford a car or go by taxi. Parts of cities such as Jerusalem are blocked off from Friday evening to Saturday evening because traffic is prohibited on Shabbat. People cannot get buried without a religious ceremony led by a Rabbi. The word atheist does not exist in the Israeli vocabulary. (All these phenomena are based on an intellectual framework that sees Israel as a place for the conservation and preservation of Judaism, which in turn is understood as a genetic, ethnic and religious category). All this supports the ghetto mentality of the Diaspora, which is one of the reasons why Jews have survived for thousand of years, but which it is now dispensable in Israel. The Israeli national idea is based on the principle of a racial segregation, isolation, fear and mistrust towards the non-Jews. Israel isolates itself from the others and is much less accepted in the Western world than it was 20 years ago," Professor Eva Ilus wrote in *Haaretz* on November 22, 2013.

Israel is an ethnocratic society

"Israel is an ethnocratic society that is imitating apartheid South Africa more and more. ... What is called in Hebrew 'Yihud'—judify—means to turn as many Israeli areas as possible into exclusive Jewish centers. This happens especially in the Galilee in the North and in the Negev in the South of Israel. The native Arab or Bedouin population is moved away, and new Israeli cities and villages spring up in the same place. (...) The biggest obstacle to a democratic Israeli society is the momentum of ethnic colonial domination. (...) The anti-liberal religious powers are deepening the Messianic and racist rhetoric and they are deepening the historical and mythical points of view as the cradle of Jewish identity." Professor Oren Yiftahel wrote in *Haaretz* on December 7, 2013

More and more Israeli journalists write with sorrow that Israel follows in the footsteps of an 'apartheid regime.' "Israel does not have the right to mourn Nelson Mandela because, unlike South Africa, the Israeli regime does not even try to stop apartheid," writes Gideon Levy. Another journalist, Amira Hess, writes about the "two different legal systems in the West Bank—the Jews are under civil law, the Palestinians are under military law, which allows the army to confiscate their land and houses in the name of security. The land is subsequently often given to settlers. The restriction list is endless," she wrote in the opinion section of *Haaretz* on December 9, 2013

Mosab, Son of Hamas[325]

"My name is Mosab Hassan Jousef. I was born near Ramallah in 1978 and am the son of Sheikh Hassan Jousef Halil, one of the seven founders of Hamas. My family is religious. My father studied advanced Islamic Studies first in Jerusalem, then in Jordan. When he arrived in Jordan in the mid-1970s, the Muslim Brotherhood had their headquarters there and did a lot of charity work. He never saw the brutal side of Islam.

When I was seven years old, my family moved to a refugee camp, one of nineteen in the West Bank, where my father became the imam of the camp. I am a son of this region, of Islam and of an evil terrorist. I'm also a believer in Jesus Christ. I took part in the Intifada. I was a prisoner in the worst jail in Israel; and in the end I became a betrayer in the eyes of the people I loved.

In 1986, Hamas was founded in Hebron. My father was there. People initially only threw stones and burned tires, but all these activities have turned into a movement that poses a real threat to Israel. My father was arrested many times, and when he returned in 1990, the Occupied Territories had become a lawless jungle. Hamas was an idea, a nightmare that could not be eradicated. After Yitzhak Rabin was assassinated, it was clear to me that Jewish fanatics and Hamas had the same goal.

In the Israeli jail, the Palestinians judged with all brutality everybody who was suspected of working for the Israeli secret service. They used to torture suspects. Israeli authorities did not do anything to stop it. A few were even murdered in jail. As the son of a Hamas leader, I was above suspicion. In 1996 I was recruited to work for the Israelis. I began studying for a BA at the university at their cost. What the Israelis taught me was much more logical and true than anything I ever heard from my own people.

The Hamas leaders came with their $70,000 cars. They were constantly planning terror attacks against Israel. Arabs all over the world burned American and Israeli flags and pumped billions of dollars into fighting against the occupation. Attacks were planned against the Israeli civil population and they succeeded in killing and injuring many Israelis.

Our enemies are ideas, and you cannot bomb ideas; in 2005, I stopped working for the Israelis and left the Middle East. I lost my family, my friends and my home."

Conclusion

Israel Is a Foreign Entity in the Middle East. Will It Always Stay This Way?

The Arab Point of View

Israel is the nearest and most comfortable geographical target for Arab terrorists, which makes the country a vulnerable "soft aim." Terrorists also know that an explosion in Israel affects the Western world less than a bomb in any European or American city. The
Arab countries surrounding Israel, which started wars against Israel in 1948, 1967, and 1973, each have their own individual interests at heart. They never intended to create an independent Palestinian state.

Palestine may become an Arabic democracy. Most likely, an independent democratic Palestine would shake up the entire Arab world and its feudal systems and totalitarian regimes. Therefore, Arab countries can obviously not be in favor of such a development because their elites would lose their privileges. The poor masses obviously do not have a say as they are constantly brainwashed to hate Israel. Arabs will denounce Israel as a common enemy for as long as they can because this gives them a certain kind of cohesion. What most Arab leaders want is not a Palestinian state but an official reason to fight Israel.

The Palestinian people have been kept hostage in Arab countries where they were seeking refuge, and can always be agitated to fight Israel.

The Israeli-Palestinian Situation

"The ongoing war between Israel and Palestine has its roots in a terrible historical tragedy experienced by the Jews, for which the population of Palestine has had to pay. Both sides still have to make the greatest efforts to end this tragedy. This can only be done through mutual understanding,"[326] Uri Avneri, Israel's Don Quixote, has stated again and again since 1948.

Palestinian-Arabs and Israeli-Jews actually depend on each other. Most countries would prefer if they didn't exist, yet they are bound together because of a historical event that established the acute need for a Jewish state after World War II. The need for a Palestinian state is urgent, and as mentioned, the paradox of history is that the only country capable of helping birth a Palestinian state is Israel. One should also not forget that ending the occupation benefits Israel as well. Israel has to understand that seeking a two-state solution is in its own interest because it makes this part of the world a place worthwhile to live in. Abu-Lughhod is "concerned with the pragmatic forces in Europe that helped in the materialization of the Zionist vision in a particular terrain. ... The legal right to do so has to be internationally recognized."[327] Savir writes, "Both parties are engaged in a 'cultural conflict' and obviously are not able to overcome practical and emotional barriers."[328]

The Arab-Israelis as well as the Palestinians in the territories have shown time and again that when conflicts such as the Golf War happen, they stand behind Israel's enemies.[329] As a result, the prestige of the moderates has declined and fanatic Islamic groups have surged, thus giving Israel reason not to trust Palestinians in general.

The Israeli-Palestinian Point of View

Enemies often do not speak the same language. They fear and distrust each other. All this becomes exacerbated when they also follow two different religions. Both Israelis and Palestinians have only each other to talk to as they try to solve one of the biggest disputes of our time. Nobody else could or should solve it for them. With all respect to European and American attempts, in the end it is up to the two parties involved to resolve the conflict.

The Palestine Liberation Army (PLO) has not been talking about the destruction of Israel but about a 'two-state solution' since 1988. On the Israeli side, most Israelis see "a two-state solution" as the only possible option. The big handicaps beside the mistrust and fear are the influence of religious powers, the Israeli settlements, as well as the indifference and ineptitude of the politicians on both sides.

An important issue is also money and economic interests of other countries in the region as well as outside of the region. Neither the Israelis nor the Palestinians emerge victorious when they pump all their resources into an armed conflict. People on both sides must become aware that there is no other choice than a peaceful one. There is no urgent need for Israelis and Palestinians to like each other—and it cannot happen immediately after all these years of brainwashing, but there is an urgent requirement to meet the essential needs of both peoples by giving everybody the chance to live a normal life without daily fears, threats and death.

The Entire Land, a Fixed Idea

Ma'har el-Hasin wrote in *el-Ahd* in 2011: "Palestine is Palestine. A Palestinian state will be different, because it is only a part of the historic Palestine, but this is what we can get and we should start to get used to it." The same holds true for the Israeli claim to the entire land. The present facts show two people have to make compromises in order to stop the conflict and start a normal life in peace.

Israel must understand that the occupation is bad for everybody, even for its people. The Israeli government has to stop religious parties from causing more damage, as they are not even members in the current coalition. Israel is morally obliged to put an end to this no-win situation without further delay, in the interest of its own people as well as in the interest of the Palestinian people.

The Palestinians on their side should find a leader willing and politically able to talk with Israel without being threatened by his or her own people. As it looks now, Israel is the only partner the Palestinians have, and the Palestinians are the only partner Israel has. Both sides should stop thinking that somebody else will solve their problems.

Both Palestinian and Israelis have to deal with religious radicals, Muslims and Jews, who have obscure reasons for not engaging in peace talks and do not want to cede one centimeter of land to the enemy, even though they themselves have never picked up arms against the Palestinians. Most Palestinians and most Israelis see the two-state solution as preferable and even desirable.

Returning Territories

After the Six-Day War of 1967, Israel offered to return the West Bank to King Hussein of Jordan, but he refused to take the region back. When Israel gave the Sinai Peninsula back to Egypt as part of the peace agreement of 1979, the Egyptian government refused to take back the Gaza Strip. A Palestinian state was never part of any agreement between Israel and its neighbors. Only after the War of 1967 did the Palestinians begin to struggle for a national identity and independence.

The question why this struggle started just as the Palestinians came under Israeli occupation is related to the fact that Palestinians knew that under an Arab regime, they would not stand a chance to achieve this goal. In Arab countries, Palestinians have been tolerated as guests and might be thrown out if they agitate for Palestinian independence.

The idea that Israel is entitled to keep the territories for security reasons will become irrelevant once a peace treaty is signed. Besides, borders have never been real barriers for people who wanted to cross them and attack civilians on the other side, as the case of Gaza has shown. The wall of concrete and wire on the 1967 border between the West Bank and Israel has not curbed the number of terrorist attacks on Israel.[330]

Israel cannot give the territories back to the Palestinians because they never belonged to them, but it can and must understand that a Palestinian state is in its own interest.

Everybody Is Guilty

The Israelis made almost every possible mistake in dialoguing and not dialoguing with the Palestinians because for decades—under the governments of Ben Gurion, Golda Meir and others— they believed that a "status quo" was in Israel's favor.

The Palestinians on their side made many mistakes by believing that the Arab countries were their partners. This is why for years only the cannon spoke in the Middle East. The truth is that Israel could never facilitate the return of all the Palestinian refugees, just like no European country would have taken back all the Jewish refugees even if they had wanted to return.

From 1967 until now, Israelis as well as Palestinians missed every possible opportunity to sign an agreement because they have yielded to the influence of religious radicals on both sides and fear political consequences, as Yitzhak Rabin's assassination tragically showed. Culture, tradition and religion have created two societies that think traditionally and act completely differently. Political sanity left the Middle East a long time ago. It is still written in the stars if it will ever return.

A Possible Solution

Peace and a 'two-state solution' are the only possible option for Israel and the Palestinians. Savir writes that it is not diplomacy that leads to peace, but the people.[331] Even if this is true, it will take decades of hard educational work to eliminate the hatred and suspicions between the two nations after all these years of brainwashing. Of course Israel and Palestine do not trust each other, but nobody else trusts the others in the Middle East either. The so-called "Cold Peace" with Egypt shows that a peace strategy should be decided from above; and, even if it is not the best, a Cold Peace is still preferable to a war. There will never be security in the region without peace. The international community, the United States, the European Union, Russia, and wealthy Arab nations should work together with Israel and Palestine to reduce, and in the long run to eliminate, the negative stereotypes and to find a common language instead of supplying weapons. They must help the region—especially the Palestinians—not by donating money, which is often misused in shady investments and corruption, but by building schools, hospitals, training teachers and doctors, and establishing an economic infrastructure so the Palestinians will one day be able to start a life of their own without depending on others for their most basic needs.

Is a Solution Impossible?

As Israel is becoming more and more isolated, it quarrels with its best friends and its biggest supporters. It is obvious that Benjamin Netanyahu uses Iran as an excuse to not engage in talks with the Palestinians as well as to sideline domestic problems. Yuval Diskin, the former chief of the Israeli Security Services Shabac, estimates that "prolonging the conflict with the Palestinians is much more dangerous for Israel than an Iranian nuclear threat." In his opinion, "Prime Minister Netanyahu is an anti-leader. He makes decisions about the Palestinians only when pressured by the United States, and only when he sees no other option. Without a clear American plan for new borders he will avoid any progress," he wrote in an editorial in *Haaretz* on December 6, 2013. The Israeli politicians ignore the need for a dialogue by using the traditional magic word *bitahon*—security—and they keep building settlements.

This megalomania, mixed with the Jewish/Israeli belief that "after the Sho'a—the Holocaust— the world owes us," (i.e. that the world will always be on our side), is dangerous to the very existence of Israel. Netanyahu is well connected to Israel's moneyed elite and to the religious radicals who want to get more funding for their Yeshivas and exhaust the country's resources by living on social welfare in the West Bank forever. Religious pressure in Israel is enormous and it influences even the most private of spheres. Since the murder of Yitzhak Rabin twenty years ago, Israel has had a right-wing government, and everybody who speaks out against the occupation is called as "leftist," which is almost a swear word.

"McCarthyism is working very well even in the high court. No court dares to condemn governmental decisions against people involved in creating new illegal settlements on Palestinian soil. The cracks in Israeli democracy are getting deeper and deeper. Nationalistic and racist laws are being put into place all the time. Apartheid measures taken against Arabs are shameful. Israeli society is becoming more right-wing, nationalistic and racialized every day. The hope for a political regularization vanishes as well," Gideon Levi wrote in the opinion section of *Haaretz* on November 11, 2013. Israeli politicians forget to whom they are committed and for whom they carry responsibility—namely the people that live in the country, 80 percent of whom are secular Jews and Arabs.

Israel is already much more isolated than it was ten or twenty years ago. The pro-Israel lobby worldwide is shrinking because the pro-Israel arguments are becoming more and more tenuous.

Israel carries the main responsibility for the peace process because it is the stronger partner.

Should the soil of Israel and Palestine be drenched in blood forever? It is time to wake up and ask who the winner of the conflict is—who wants the war and why. Who benefits from war the most? Neither Israelis nor Palestinians are among the winners: they both are on the losing end.

You know how strong your ties to a country are when its policy annoys and angers you and makes you feel helpless. This is how I feel about Israel.

Foot Notes

---

[1] Shlaim, pp. 2, 53.

[2] In the time between the two World Wars, only a relatively small number of Jews made "aliyah," immigration to Israel, although there were many Zionist organizations all over Europe. Zionism was a theoretical idea because the imminent danger of Nazi persecution was not yet visible. To a great extent, the world Jewry supported the "Yishuv" — the Jewish community in Palestine before the foundation of the state of Israel in 1948 in Palestine. Herzl, Douer, *Neuland*, Article Anderl, p. 43-48.

[3] Rabinovich, *Peace*, p. 14.

[4] Shamir, *Modern History*, p. 201.

[5] *Encyclopedia Britannica*, eleventh edition, 1911.

[6] Foster, p. 10-12.

[7] The East Bank of the river Jordan, which also belonged to the Damascus province, was divided into Agaloon and Charach. Shamir, *Modern History*, p. 9.

[8] Commander of the army of Muhammad Ali (1769-1849), King of Egypt.

[9] One year later they conquered Damascus. pp. 49, 203-204.

[10] Shamir, *Modern History*, pp. 49, 73.

[11] Carl S. Ehrlich "Philistines" *The Oxford Guide to People and Places of the Bible*. Ed.: Bruce M. Metzger and Michael D. Coogan, Oxford University Press, 2001.

[12] Sand, p. 27. Shlomo Sand is a professor at Tel Aviv University.

[13] Sand, p. 37-38.

[14] Khalidi, p. 205.

[15] Sakhanini, p. 175-178. Halil Sakhanini is a Palestinian intellectual who lives in Jerusalem.

[16] Muslim invasion: 642, Umayyad 661-750, Abbasid 750-914, Fatimid 914-1171, Ayyubid 1171-1250/1341, Mamluk 1250-1517, Ottoman 1517-1917. *Encyclopedia of Islam*. Volume VII. Encyclopedia Judaica, Volume 6, „Ancient Egypt", S. 222-223.

[17] Nasser, p. 41.

[18] Karmi, pp. 64, 69-70, 73.

[19] Genesis: 13;13, 14;7,15;8 to Abraham, 26;3 to Isaac, 28;13, 35;12 to Jacob, who changes his name to Israel 35;10.

[20] The Prophet said, "I was taken on a journey by night to "Bayt al-Maqdis". They said, "Aelia." He replied, "Yes." al-Bukhārī 2000, v.2: 956; Muslim 2000, v.1: 88, al-Ṭabarānī nd, v.12:167-8; Ibn Abī Shaybah 1994, v.7:422-3, v.8:445; Ibn 'Asākir 1996, v.41:235, El-Awaisi, p. 5.

[21] A complete translation can be found in El-Awaisi (2005:72-74).

[22] El-Khatib, p. 26-27.

[23] Goitein, p. 9-11.

[24] Goitein, p. 220.

[25] Goitein, p. 220.

[26] Shamir, *Modern History*, p. 276-278.

[27] Shamir, *Modern History*, p. 206-208.

[28] In the mid-7th century with the annexation of the Middle East, the Arab peninsula, North Africa as well as Spain and Portugal. Shamir, *Modern History*, p. 280.

[29] About a quarter of the 86,000 Jews of Palestine had to leave the country. Shamir, *Modern History*, p. 293.

[30] Shamir, *Modern History*, p. 293.

[31] Goitein, p. 215.

[32] Lord Arthur James Balfour (1848-1930), British Foreign Minister from 1916 to 1919. The declaration was handed down from Lord Balfour on behalf of the British government to Lord Rothschild as the representative of the Zionist Federation. Nahem, article Jerushalmi, p. 119. Robert John, *Behind the Balfour Declaration. Britain's Great War Pledge To Lord Rothschild.* Published by the Institute for Historical Review, 1988.

[33] Shamir, *Modern History*, p. 300.

[34] Weizmann was a representative of the Jews abroad, later chief of the Jewish Congress; he took part in all but the first Zionist congresses in Basel, Switzerland. He served as the first Israeli president from 1949 until his death in 1952.

[35] Balfour Declaration. Lord Arthur James Balfour (1848-1930), British Prime Minister. 1916-1919 Minister of Foreign affairs in a letter to Lord Rothschild: "... His Majesty's government views with favour the establishment in Palestine of a national home for the Jewish people..." Nahem, article Jerushalmi, p. 119. Robert John. *Behind the Balfour Declaration. Britain's Great War. Pledge To Lord Rothschild.* Published by the Institute for Historical Review, 1988. Douer: *Egypt*, p. 121. Kraemer, p. 172. Abu-Lughhod, p. 60.

[36] White Book, also White Paper: a policy paper issued by the British government with suggestions for a solution to the problems in Palestine.

[37] Some 56,000 Jews lived in Palestine in 1917, compared to about 600,000 Arabs. Shlaim, p. 29-33.

[38] The Zion Mule Corps was established in 1915 under the command of Joseph Trumpeldor (1880-1920); the corps fought side by side with the British army during World War I in Gallipoli. It is considered the first all-Jewish military unit in about two thousand years of Jewish history.

[39] During World War I, the number of Jews in Israel increased from 65,000 to 85,000. Rupin, p. 146-147, Ben-Gavriel, p. 40-41.

[40] Jabotinsky, *Documents*. Shlaim, p. 35-38.

[41] Ben-Gurion emigrated to Eretz Israel in 1906. He headed the Israeli government and was Defense Minister until 1963. Shlaim a.o.

[42] Ben Gurion, Meetings, p. 85.

[43] The phenomenon of dividing countries after wars has also been practiced in other parts of the world such as Yugoslavia (after World War II), Africa and in South America.

[44] Regions under Mandate were not colonies but trusts in which the mandatory powers administrated territories under the supervision of the League of Nations through a special Commission. Mansfield, p. 195-196.

[45] Moris, p. 24-25. Benny Moris, born 1948 in Israel. A former journalist, Moris now is professor of Middle Eastern history at Ben Gurion University of Beer Sheba. He wrote many books about the Israeli-Palestinian question. He is a key member of a group of Israeli historians known as the "New Historians," who criticize Israeli politics and the occupation. Avi Shlaim, Ilan Pappe and others also belong to this group.

[46] Amos Elon, *The New York Book Review*, December 19, 1996. Amos Elon (1926, Vienna – 2009, Jerusalem), writer, correspondent for *Haaretz*, fellow at New York University School of Law. Elon was one of the earliest advocates for the creation of a Palestinian state and withdrawal from the Occupied Territories. Elon rose to international fame in the early 1970s after publishing *The Israelis: Founders and Builders*, one of the earliest books on the subject.

[47] Moris, p. 28-29.

[48] Nasser, p. 13-19. Nasser was born in Palestine. From 1962 to 1964 he wrote this book, which is full of hatred and accusations towards Jews, Zionism, Britain, the United States, and the United Nations, over the fate of the Palestinians.

[49] (1171-1250) Douer, *Ägypten*, p. 63-66.

[50] (1250-1517) Douer, *Ägypten*, p. 76-79.

[51] Douer, *Ägypten*, p. 120-122.

[52] Said, *Politics*, p. xiii. Like many other intellectuals who do not live in the region, Edward Said was also against Arab-Israeli peace talks. Said, *Dispossession*, p. 34-35.

[53] Shlaim, p. 41-45.

[54] Moris, p. 15.

[55] Article: Amos Elon, in *The New York Book Review*. December 19, 1996.

[56] Starting in 1936, the Arab population of Palestine organized strikes and violent rebellions, demanding an end to Jewish immigration and a ban on real estate sales to Jews. In May of 1939, the British Mandatory Authority issued a White Paper that limited immigration to a minimum. Douer, *Neuland*, article Anderl, p. 43-48,

[57] May 28, 2009, Donald MacIntyre, *The Independent*, London.

[58] Milton Goldin Tarrytown, N.Y., June 24, 1988. July 8, 1988 *The New York Times*, opinion section.

[59] Aliyah means "ascent" in Hebrew. This movement existed for centuries and was closely tied to a striving for Zion, one of the main tenets of Jewish religion.

The Zionist "First Aliyah" movement started in Europe in the 1880s and went on until the 1930s. See Scharfstein, p. 231.

[60] There were about 24,000 Jews in Palestine in 1882. Bein, p. 9.

[61] Moris, p. 18.

[62] Bein, p. 29

[63] Yishuv means settlement in Hebrew and denotes the Jewish minority that lived in Palestine until 1948.

[64] Dunam: 1000 square meters.

[65] Sursuq sold another 70,000 Dunam in 1920. Kraemer, p. 135-141, Bein, p. 216-217.

[66] Moris, p. 18.

[67] Emir Feisal, member of the Hashemite dynasty. He was King of Greater Syria in 1920, then King of Iraq from 1921 to 1933.

[68] Feisal was at the time the authorized agent of the National Arab Movement in Palestine. Bein, p. 330.

[69] Olim: Hebrew: ascendants. Immigrants to Palestine, later Israel.

[70] The exact numbers of Olim cannot be determined. According to the report of the 15th Zionist Congress of 1927, there were 37,345 people making alyiah, according to the report of the Jewish Agency, 35,000. Bein, p. 185.

[71] The acquired land has remained in the hand of the Israeli government to this day and is leased out for housing, agricultural purposes and the like. Bein, p. 220-222.

[72] Political differences between the Jewish parties on what Israel needed were added to all the existing problems. Bein, p. 223-224.

[73] Halutzim means “pioneers” in Hebrew.

[74] Tel Aviv was the home of Jewish and British institutions and a center for the construction, textile, and printing industries. The region’s first power grid was also set up there. Many shops, small industries, hotels, and restaurants opened after Tel Aviv was founded. Bein, p. 263-4.

[75] Haifa was chosen mostly because of the Carmel Mountains and its climate. Bein, p. 263-4.

[76] Hebron was one of the oldest Jewish centers in Palestine. After this massacre, Hebron did not have a Jewish population until 1967, after the Six-Day War. Bein, p. 331-3.

[77] Abu-Lughhod, Article John Ruedy, Georgetown University, p. 129-134.

[78] Falah means “peasant” in Arabic.

[79] The peasants “lost” the land in which they had lived and worked for generations because Jews had legally bought it from the peasants’ Arab landlords who did not care about what would happen to them.

[80] Later, in the early 1940s, the Nazi idea of eliminating the Jews became a reality and Jews had to flee. The ones who did not manage to get outside of Nazi-dominated territory ended up in concentration camps and later on in death camps where they were murdered.

[81] These efforts culminated in the Balfour Declaration on November 2, 1917, issued by the British Foreign Minister of the same name who was in favor of creating a home for the Jews within Palestine. Abu-Lughhod, p. 7, article Stevens, p. 50-56.

[82] In 1927, not a single Jewish person immigrated to Palestine, in 1928 only ten people. The situation changed in 1929 when Zionist—mostly from outside of the region—enlarged the Jewish Agency. This caused the first Arab revolt with many casualties on both sides. Mansfield, p. 204.

[83] Film: *Jews & Muslims*. Director: Emanuel Blanchare, Arte, 2013.

[84] Mainly due to Hitler’s rise to power in Germany, Jewish immigration to Palestine rose sharply, in 1930 to 4,000, in 1933 to 30,000, and in 1935 to 62,000, in spite of all the restrictions imposed by the British Mandate. Mansfield, p. 205-206.

[85] Hilel Cohen. *What Really Happened in 1929?* News release, Evrit and Keter Publishers, 2013. Book review, Dalia Karpel, *Haaretz*, October 25, 2013.

[86] Moris, p. 27.

[87] Ben-Gavriel, p. 50.

[88] More than 600 Jews were killed, over 1,000 wounded and a substantial amount of property was destroyed. Bein, p. 366-7.

[89] Film: *Jews & Muslims*. Director: Emanuel Blanchare, Arte, 2013.

[90] The only exception was "Youth Aliyahh", in which children from age 8 to 18 were sent to Great Britain, Sweden, Holland, and Denmark. They were exceptionally allowed into Eretz Israel/Palestine by the British.

[91] In many cases, Jews only left for Palestine if they had no other choice. Douer, *Neuland*, article Niederland, p. 49-53.

[92] About 29 percent came from Germany in 1936. By 1939, this number rose to 71 percent. Jews were only allowed to immigrate to the British Mandate zone if they possessed a certificate, a kind of visa: a "capitalist certificate," if they could prove that they owned the stately sum of 1,000 pounds, or a "student certificate," which was awarded to talented secondary school and university students who were selected by emissaries of the British Mandatory Authorities. Wives, children and parents of certificate holders needed "category D" certificates. There were also a small number of "quota" immigrants who were let into the country by the authorities every year. The exact number of European Jews coming to the region is not known, and there were also people that immigrated illegally. Kraemer, p. 308-9. Bein, p. 343.

[93] Moris, p. 441.

[94] Ben-Gavriel, p. 53.

[95] For most European Jews, Palestine was the last possible alternative to escape concentration camps and death by the National Socialists. *Neuland*, Anderl, p. 43-48.

[96] *Neuland*, Douer, Introduction p. 39-42.

[97] Aliyah Bet: The code name for the illegal immigration to Israel that occurred between 1934 and 1948 in violation of the British White Paper restrictions. Ha'apala - Hebrew: ascension.

[98] Most of the newcomers were from Austria, Germany and the Czech Republic. Almost 20,000 people made aliyah illegally from 1939 to 1945 and about 15,000 from 1945 to 1948. Moris, p. 47, Bein, P.368-9, 386.

[99] Ben-Gavriel, p. 64.

[100] Yishuv: The Jewish population of Palestine until the state of Israel was founded in 1948.

[101] Sohnut: The Jewish Agency, a non-profit Jewish organization founded in Jaffa in 1908. This organization was responsible for the immigration and integration of the people who had made *aliyah*. See Abu-Lughhod, Kraemer, Bein.

[102] The Peel Commission was founded in 1936 by the British government to research and offer solutions to the problems between Arabs and Jews in Palestine. The Commission found it necessary to create two different states—an Arab and a Jewish one—with each population moving to their respective territory. Most

Jewish leaders agreed although they did not like the idea. The Arab leadership did not agree. Bein, p. 370, Abu-Lughhod, Article Verdery, p. 298-299. See also Kraemer, Moris, Bein, Ben-Gavriel, p. 54.

[103] Moris, p. 35.

[104] Peel Commission: A royal commission to solve the problems between Jews and Arabs in Eretz Israel/Palestine. The commission suggested a division into a small Jewish state of 5,000 square kilometers. The majority of the land was to be given to a new Arab state and Jerusalem, which were to have access to the Mediterranean by way of Jaffa. Shlaim, p. 41-45, Moris, p. 32-34, Sand, p. 220.

[105] Mansfield, pp. 206-207, 210.

[106] Keren Kayemet, a governmental non-profit Jewish fund was founded in 1901. It aimed to buy and develop land in Eretz Israel/Palestine for Jewish settlements. Bein, p. 382-85. Kraemer, p. 135-141.

[107] In 1936, 21,300 Dunam of land were in Jewish possession. By 1947, more land was purchased, reaching 450,000 Dunam. Bein, p. 382-5. Kraemer, p. 135-141.

[108] Abu-Lughhod, article John Reudy, p. 133.

[109] The British Authorities had selected al-Hussayni as Mufti. He was an Arab scholar of Islam until 1922. He then became Grand Mufti of Jerusalem. He was elected President of the Supreme Muslim Council. During World War II, he established ties to the Axis powers. In 1941 he went to Europe and met with Hitler. Kupferschmidt, pp. 19, 78, Moris, p. 27.

[110] Istiqlal – Arabic: "Independent (Party)" established in 1932, a strongly nationalistic party.

[111] The Party of the mufti re-appeared in 1944. His Hajj entrance to Israel was declined and so he remained in exile. Smith, p. 181.

[112] Moris, p. 36.

[113] Ben-Gavriel, p. 61.

[114] The Cold War between the East and the West was actually between the Soviet Union and the United States. See also Smith, p. 184-85.

[115] History shows that Jews would not have left Europe to go to the desert if they had not been forced to. The same happened with Jews of the Arab countries who were expelled or threatened after 1948 and only then started to leave their countries of origin.

[116] Yoram Kaniuk, in: Itamar Kremer, *Haaretz*, June 13, 2013

[117] Sand, p. 30-31.

[118] Moris, pp. 37, 83.

[119] Moris, p. 40.

[120] Smith, p. 202-03, Kraemer, p. 375-77, Sand, p. 232.

[121] Kraemer, p. 362. The partition plan of November 29, 1947 was decided by a majority of 66 percent of all members. The General Assembly proposed a Jewish state with 498,000 Jewish and 407,000 Arab inhabitants, and an Arab state with 725,000 Arab and 10,000 Jewish inhabitants. Abu-Lughhod, p. 380-84.

[122] Shlaim, pp. 47-48, 56-57.

[123] From the speech of Rabbi Hillel Silver "Testimony on Zionist Reaction" (to the partition) to the UNSCOP proposals October 2, 1947. Smith, p. 222, Moris, p. 56-57.

[124] Mansfield, p. 235.

[125] Mansfield, p. 235.

[126] Kraemer, p. 361.

[127] Moris, p. 42.

[128] Mutawi, Samir. *Jordan in the 1967 War*. Cambridge, 1987.

[129] 45 percent of the land was to be Arab, 55 percent Jewish. Sand, p. 229-230.

[130] Mansfield, p. 235-236.

[131] Shlaim, p. 51-52.

[132] Moris, pp. 95-97, 133, Abu-Lughhod, Article Waines, p. 231-235.

[133] Abu-Lughhod, p. 381.

[134] Shlaim, p. 303.

[135] Kraemer, p. 363-4.

[136] Kraemer, p. 366-67.

[137] Abu-Lughhod, article Ruedy, p. 136-37.

[138] Kraemer, p. 368. Abu-Lughhod, article Hudson, p. 317.

[139] Kr Moris, p. 34-35.

[140] Moris, p. 116-117.

[141] Cohen, Palestine, p. 306.

[142] Although the latter was separated from the rest by a decision of the British in 1922.

[143] Hugi, p. 31-32. Jacky Hugi is an Israeli radio and newspaper journalist and professor of journalism in Tel Aviv.

[144] Moris, p. 430-431.

[145] Moris, p. 84-88.

[146] Moris, p. 89.

[147] See: Kraemer, Abu-Lughhod, Smith and others.

[148] See also Stevens.

[149] Although they were never an official group and never considered themselves as such, Israeli historians Benni Moris, Avi Schleim, Tom Segev and others are considered the New Historians because they wrote about the same subject at almost the same time.

[150] Moris, p. 431-437.

[151] Moris, p. 425.

[152] Moris, p. 426-428.

[153] Moris, p. 429-430.

[154] Kraemer, p. 369.

[155] Shlaim, p. 54-60.

[156] In April of 1950, Jordan annexed the West Bank. Shlaim, p. 82.

[157] Rabinovich, 1991, p. 290.

[158] Moris, p. 451.

[159] Moris, pp. 95, 204-208, 425.

[160] Sharet, government protocol of February 9, 1949.

[161] Said, *Politics*, pp. 136-7, 163-4.

[162] Hadawi, p. 128.

[163] Sand, p. 230-231.

[164] Abu-Lughhod, article Ruedy, p. 136-7.

[165] Kraemer, Moris, Shimoni a. o.

[166] Abu-Lughhod: article Childers, p. 181-182.

[167] Smith, p. 207.

[168] Nasser, p. 107.

[169] Nasser, p. 155.

[170] Moris, p. 444-447.

[171] Moris, p. 443.

[172] Arieli, p. 440.

[173] Nasser, p. 49-55.

[174] Interview with Said, London *Sunday Times*, June 19, 1977.

[175] For understandable reasons I cannot give the names of this interviewee. Rabinovich, *Peace*, p. 222.

[176] Goitein, p. 237-238.

[177] Smith, p. 202-3, Kraemer, p. 375-77, Sand, p. 232.

[178] Perez, p. 151, Abu-Lughhod: article Childers, p. 185.

[179] Abu-Lughhod: article Ruedy, p. 138.

[180] Arieli, p. 422.

[181] Smith, p. 477.

[182] As of today, most of the Palestinians who fled to Arab countries still live in refugee camps, and the question of how their situation should be resolved remains one of the most pressing issues in the Israeli-Palestinian conflict.

[183] UNRWA is a United Nations organization dedicated to aid and support Palestinian refugees in the Middle East.

[184] Benedict, p. 391-392.

[185] Hadawi, p. 139.

[186] Many Jewish refugees arrived by boat. Jews from Yemen, Persia, Aden, and later from Iraq arrived by planes in the Night and Fog directives. See also Bein, p. 390.

[187] Kraemer, p. 360.

[188] Moris, p. 43.

[189] Arieli, p. 221.

[190] Eli Avidar (Abudra) was born in Egypt. An Orientalist who served at the Israeli Ministry of Foreign Affairs and an Israeli representative in Qatar, he is the founder and chairman of The Smart Middle East

Forum. Avidar is also a Middle East analyst for Arab Israeli and foreign media. He lives by the motto "The Palestinian people are not our enemy." Avidar, pp. 136-137, 150.

[191] Steinberg, pp. 23-24, 196.

[192] Arieli, p. 432.

[193] Hadawi, p. 135.

[194] Benedict, pp. 48-49, 259.

[195] Benedict, p. 394-395.

[196] Benedict, p.2 60-262. Hans Benedict was a special correspondent for the Austrian television ORF in the Middle East in the late 1970s and 1980s.

[197] Perez, p. 99. Smith, p. 229.

[198] Abu-Lughhod, Article Waines, p. 207.

[199] Nahem, article Ehrlich, p. 25, Shlaim, p. 152-157, 172, Kraemer, p. 221.

[200] Shlaim, p. 170-176, 184-189.

[201] Abu-Lughhod, article Hudson, p. 333-5. See also Kerr, p. 140-152.

[202] Kerr, p. 169.

[203] Abu-Lughhod, Article Hudson, p. 336.

[204] This reminds me of the Austrian relief project for Yugoslavia: Nachbar in Not (Neighbor in Need). Money and goods were collected during the war so that people in the region would not cross the border.

[205] A letter from the chairman of the UN Conciliation Commission for Palestine on the position of the Palestinian refugees. November 17, 1949. Smith, p. 260

[206] Chittick, p. 33.

[207] Chittick, p. 33.

[208] Kedourie, Eli: *The Arab-Israeli Conflict*. London, 1974 p. 218-213. Shamir, Shimon: The Arab-Israeli Conflict. In: A. L. Udovich: *The Middle East: Oil, Conflict and Hope*. Lexington, Mas, 1976. p. 195-231.

[209] Rabinovich, 1991, p. 13.

[210] Said, *Politics*, p. xvii.

[211] Said, *Politics*, p. 6.

[212] Said, *Politics*, p. 29.

[213] Hadawi, p. 149-152.

[214] One should not forget that the average annual income in Israel is $18,000; in Palestine $1,000. Rabinovich, 2012, p. 324. Besides, Israeli Arabs are used to living in a democracy and would not want to return to a totalitarian Arab regime.

[215] Article by Arnon Soffer and Gil Shalev: "The De-Facto Implementation of the Palestinian Request of Return." Arieli, p. 423-425.

[216] Jordan was the only Arab state to offer refugees full citizenship. King Abdullah of Jordan was assassinated by a young Palestinian man in Jerusalem in 1951. Mansfield, p. 240.

[217] Rabinovich, 1991, p. 20.

[218] For an exact evaluation of mainstream thinking in Israel see Amos Oz, *Here and There in Eretz Israel*, Am Oved Publishers, Tel Aviv 1982.

[219] *The New York Times*, December 19, 2002.

[220] May 28, 2009, Donald Macintyre, *The Independent*, London.

[221] Sand, pp. 238-241, 245.

[222] *The New York Times*, December 19, 2002.

[223] Mansfield, p. 275.

[224] Said, *Politics*, p. 137-8.

[225] Benedict, p. 337.

[226] Rabinovich, 2012, p. 298-300.

[227] Rabinovich, Peace, p. 22.

[228] Rabinovich, 1991, p. 28-29.

[229] Mansfield, p. 307.

[230] Shlaim, p. 479.

[231] President Mubarak of Egypt, King Hussein of Jordan, the foreign ministers of Oman, Qatar, Tunisia, and Morocco came from the Arab world. American President Clinton and King Hussein gave a eulogy for Yitzak Rabin. Yasser Arafat wanted to come, but was asked to stay home for security reasons. He later paid his last respects to Rabin's widow and told her, "I lost a friend." She refused to shake hands with Netanyahu because of his part in the agitation that led to the murder of her husband. Shlaim, p. 511-513.

[232] Ajami, p. 281.

[233] *The New York Times,* Dec 21, 1995, Jerusalem.

[234] Mansfield, p. 308.

[235] Ajami, p. 243-244.

[236] Ajami, p. 246-249.

[237] Mansfield, p. 377.

[238] See the original PLO Charter.

[239] Abu-Lughhod, article Waines, p. 207.

[240] Mansfield, p. 256-257.

[241] In: "The Middle East and the Crisis of 1956" in: *St. Anthony's Papers*, no. 4, Middle Eastern Affairs, no. 1. London, 1958. p. 35.

[242] Shlaim, p. 324.

[243] Fatah: Palestinian national liberation movement.

[244] Some sources say that Fatah was established within the largest faction of the PLO by Yasser Arafat in 1959.

[245] Said, *Politics*, pp. 157-160, 165.

[246] Hamas was founded in Gaza as an extension of the Muslim Brotherhood.

[247] Rabinovich, 2012, p. 268.

[248] Rabinovich, *Peace*, pp. 52, 73.

[249] The Shia organization Hezbollah was established in Lebanon in 1982. One of its goals is to attack Israel and the West. It is supported by Syria and Iran.

[250] Lohlker, p. 246-247, Sayyid, p. 16, Kassir, p. 1f.

[251] Mansfield, p. 316-317.

[252] Rabinovich, *Peace*, pp. 39, 79. On the one side, social powers such as Rabin, Peres, Barak; on the revisionist side Shamir, Sharon, Netanyahu (whose father, a historian of the Spanish Jewry in the Middle Ages, advocated for a classical right-wing Zionist approach that has not changed to this day).

[253] Sand, p. 246.

[254] Shlaim, pp. 428, 433-434.

[255] Ajami, pp. 9, 40.

[256] These numbers cannot be verified. In interviews in the United States with Palestinians who wanted to remain anonymous, a Palestinian minority of about half a million people settled in Detroit.

[257] Arieli, p. 406-408.

[258] Said, *Politics*, p. 47.

[259] Said, *Politics*, p. 49.

[260] Said, *Politics*, p. 49-52.

[261] Said, *Politics*, p.p. 120, 126-7.

[262] Said, *Politics*, p. 6.

[263] Said, *Politics*, p. 126.

[264] See official statistics of students in Israel. When studying the geography of the Arab countries, one realizes that the Palestinians within the 1948 borders have no illiteracy rate, whereas in other Arab countries the situation is completely different, with 40 to 60 percent illiterate. The situation in the Occupied Territories changed because of mandatory education from the age of 5 to 15.

[265] Goitein, p. 237-238.

[266] I listed only the most important educational institutions.

[267] El-Mahdi, pp. 151, 207.

[268] El-Mahdi, pp 1-2, 15.

[269] Avidar, p. 125.

[270] Avidar, p. 191.

[271] Barak Ravid, *Haaretz*, January 3, 2012.

[272] Sand, pp. 246, 249.

[273] Rabinovich, *Peace*, pp. 56, 59.

[274] El-Mahdi, p. 2. El-Mahdi owns the Cairo publishing house El-Daar el-Arabia lil-Nashr, which publishes invaluable literature, also by Israeli authors. He is an independent intellectual and publicist in Cairo. Although El-Mahdi is aware of the selective democracy in Israel, he still recognizes it because of "freedom of speech, political representation, free elections and a judicial system."

[275] El-Mahdi, p. 199.

[276] Benedict, p. 391-392.

[277] "Locked in a struggle for influence of Arab public opinion, Iraq and Egypt were equally vehement in their rhetoric about upholding Arab rights in Palestine. Neither regime wished to suffer politically by making any conciliatory initiatives in the matter, even though both may have been ready to normalize relationships with Israel, and neither was capable of retrieving those rights through force." Abu-Lughhod, Article Hudson, ü. 330, 333.

[278] Said, *Politics,* p. ix- xii.

[279] Said, *Politics,* p. 20-21.

[280] Said, *Politics*, p. 139.

[281] Said, *Politics*, pp. 173, 187.

[282] Said, *Politics*, p. 234.

[283] Avidar, p. 13-15.

[284] Avidar, pp. 81, 124.

[285] Avidar, pp. 13-15, 18, 21, 31.

[286] Hugi, p. 126-129.

[287] Muhammad Sayyid Ahmed, London, 1976, pp. 67, 111.

[288] Hugi, p. 135-136.

[289] See Bill Clinton, *My Life.* New York 2004. Mahmud Abbas, *Through Secret Channels*. Reading, UK 1995 and Smith, p. 432-3.

[290] There were ten rounds of talks in Madrid. Shlaim, pp. 457-458, 544.

[291] Shamir, Israeli prime minister, 1986-1992.

[292] Shlaim, pp. 459-460, 466.

[293] Mansfield, p. 353.

[294] Shlaim, p. 482-484.

[295] The Hebron massacre of 1994, and murder of Rabin in 1995.

[296] See: Ziad Abu-Amr, *Islamic Fundamentalism in the West Bank and Gaza*. Indiana, 1994, and Hisham H. Ahmed, *The Rise of Hamas in Palestinian Society*. Jerusalem 1994.

[297] See: Josef Alpher: *What Went Wrong? The American Jewish Committee*, New York, 1998.

[298] Ajami, p. 236.

[299] Ajami, p. 253.

[300] Even Netanyahu's father, a university professor, doubted his son's integrity. Shlaim, p. 531-533.

[301] Ajami, p. 283.

[302] Shlaim, pp. 535, 544.

[303] In 1998 about 74 percent of the Jewish population of Israel supported a two-state solution, while more than 70 percent of the Palestinians still supported a peace process. Shlaim, p. 562-563.

[304] Shlaim, p. 545.

[305] Shlaim, p. 561

[306] Shlaim, p. 569.

[307] Shlaim, p. 570-571.

[308] In 2005, Ariel Sharon suffered a stroke and has not regained consciousness ever since. See: *Sharon Ariel: A Life in Times of Turmoil*. By Fredi Eytan and Robert David, Israel 2008.

[309] See: *Haaretz*, *New York Times*, *Jerusalem Post*, *Washington Post* and other newspapers on these dates.

[310] Avidar, pp. 129-130, 143-144, 154.

[311] Ajami, p. 285.

[312] Arieli, p. 277-278.

[313] Said, *Politics*, pp. 231, 238.

[314] Arieli, p. 335.

[315] Arieli, p. 480.

[316] Arieli, p. 485.

[317] Since 1947, arms expenditures alone have surpassed $25 billion and are still on the rise. Chomsky, pp. 61, 75-77.

[318] Quote: Chomsky, p. 49-50.

[319] Hadawi, p. 134.

[320] Arieli, p. 245-248.

[321] Except for the Cold Peace with Egypt since 1979 and with Jordan since 1984.

[322] Shlaim, p. 556-557.

[323] Hadawi, pp. 179-180, 189, 215, 220-221. I could not find any other evidence for this statement. Compared to other books, Hadawi's book has a very short bibliography on the subject and he hardly quotes any other author.

[324] Yehoshua, pp. 62-67, 89, 93, 99, 102.

[325] Mosab, see bibliography.

[326] Avneri, p. 10.

[327] Abu-Lughhod, pp. 4, . 6-7.

[328] Savir, p. 13.

[329] During the Gulf War, Palestinians were the only Arabs who, with the encouragement of their leader Yasser Arafat, praised and celebrated Saddam Hussein's invasion of Kuwait.

[330] Since these barriers were erected, suicide bomb attacks were reduced by 60 to 80 percent.

[331] Savir, P 22. The peace between Egypt and Israel was made in 1979 by governments, not by individuals, and although it became a "Cold Peace" it is better than a war. During my stay in Egypt in 2009, I met many Arabs that agree with me. One of them put it this way: "At least we have not had a war in 30 years."

Selected Bibliography

Abu-Amr, Ziad: *Islamic Fundamentalism in the West Bank and Gaza.* Indiana, 1994

Abu-Lughood, Ibrahim (editor): *The Transformation of Palestine: Essays.* Northwestern University Press Evanston, 1971

Abu Nowar Ma'an: *The Jordanian-Israeli War, 1948-1951.* Reading, UK: Ithaca Press, 2002

Ajami, Fouad: *The Dream Palace of the Arabs.* Am Oved Publishers, Tel Aviv, 2003

Al-Tal, Abdalla: *Memories.* Maarahot Publishers, Tel Aviv, 1960

Albaz, Sagi: *Minority Opinion in the Hebrew Press.* Dionon Publishers, Israel, 2013, Article by Ya'ir La'or (Journalist) in the *Haaretz* daily, Mai 9, 2013

Algha, J.E.: he *The Shifts in Hezbollah's Ideology: Religious Ideology, Political Ideology, and Political Program.* (ISIM dissertation) Amsterdam, 2006

Amizur, Ilan: *Embargo, Power and Decision in the 1948 War.* Ma'arahot/ Ministry of Defense Publisher, Tel Aviv, 1995

Arieli, Shaul: *A Border between Us and You.* Aliyat-Gag Publishers, Tel Aviv, 2013

Avineri, Shlomo: *Israel and the Palestinians.* New York, 1971

Avneri, Uri: *Be'sdot Pleshet, Battle Diary.* Tverski Publishers, Tel Aviv, 1949

Ayubi, N.: *Politischer Islam. Religion und Politk in der Arabischen Welt.* Freiburg, 2002

Bar-Zohar, Michael: *In Front of the Cruel Mirror: the Israeli Moment of Truth.* Yediot Aharonot Publishers, Tel Aviv, 1990

Ben Gavriel, M., Y.: *Israel, Wiedergeburt eines Staates.* R. Oldenburg, Publishers, volume 4, Germany, 1957

Ben Gurion, David:

- *Meetings with Arab Leaders.* Am Oved Publishers, Tel Aviv, 1967
- *Vision and Road.* (5 volumes). Mapai Publishers, Tel Aviv, 1951-1957

Benedict, Hans: *Kirschen aus Sidon, the Middle Eastern Conflict.* Goldmann Publishers, Wien-München, 2. Print, 1991

Bein, Dr. Alex: *History of the Jewish Settlement in Israel from Herzl until now.* Massada Publisher, Israel 1976

Ben Gurion, David: *Meetings with Arab Leaders.* Am Oved Publisher, Tel Aviv, 1975

Bennvenisti, Meron: *Sacred Landscape. The Buried History of the Holy Land since 1948.* University of California Press, Berkeley, 2000

Black, Ian and Moris, Benny: *Israel's Secret Wars: The Untold History of Israel's Intelligence Services.* Hamish Milton Publishers, London, 1991

Boutros-Ghali, Boutros: *The Arab Response to the Challenge of Israel.* In: Udovich, The Middle East: Oil, Conflict and Hope.

Campbell, John: *Defence of the Middle East.* New York, 1960

Chittick C. William: *Science of the Cosmos, Science of the Soul: The Pertinence of Islamic Cosmology in the Modern World.* Oneworld Publications, Oxford, 2007

Chomsky, Noam: *Middle East Illusions.* Rowman & Littlefield Publishers, London, 2003

Cohen, Hilel: *Army of Shadows, Palestinian Collaboration for Zionism, Intelligence, Settlements, Assassination, Policy, 1917-1948.* Hebrew Publisher, Jerusalem, 2004

Cohen, Michael: *Palestine: Retreat from the Mandate, the Making of British Policy, 1936-1945.* London, 1978

Cook, David: Tamim Al-Dari. In: Bulletin of the School of Oriental and African Studies, University of London, Nr. 1, 1998, pp. 20-28. Cambridge University Press

Dinour, Be-Zion (HG): *The History of the Haganah.* Vol. I., Jerusalem, 1954-6

Djamel, Ahmed: *War Memories of a Turkish Statesman. 1013-1919.* London, 1922

Douer, Alisa: *Neuland, Israeli Artists of Austrian Origin.* Picus Publisher, Vienna 1997

Douer, Alisa: *Ägypten – die verlorene Heimat. Der Exodus aus Ägypten, 1947-1967.* (Egypt- the Lost Home. The Exodus from Egypt, 1947-1067.) PhD dissertation. University of Vienna, 2012

Eban, Abba: *Personal Witness: Israel through my Eyes.* Putnam Publishers, New York, 1991

Efrat, Elisha: *Geography of Annexation.* Carmel Publishers, Israel, 2002

El-Awaisi, 'Abd al-Fatah: *The Muslim Brothers and the Palestine Question. 1928-1947.* I. B. Tauris Publishers, London, 1998

Eldar, Akiva & Zertal Idit: *Lords of the Land. The Settlers and the State of Israel 1967-2004.* Kinneret, Zmora-Bitan Publishers, Israel, 2004

Elon, Amos: *The Israelis.* Fritz Molden Publishers, Vienna, 1972

El-Khatib, Abdallah: Jerusalem in the Quran. British Journal of Middle Eastern Studies, 28 (1), 2001. Published online: Jun 2010

El-Mahdi, Amin: *The Other Option. In the Name of Democracy and Peace.* Introduction: Shimon Shamir. Ha'kibbutz ha'meuchad Publishers, Israel, 2001

El-Youssef, Samir: *The Illusion of Return.* Yediot Aharonot Publishers, Tel Aviv, 2008

Fawaz, Geogre: *Egypt and the 1948 War: Internal conflict and Regional Ambition.* In: Eugene L. Rogan and

Flapan, Simha: *Zionism and the Palestinians.* Croom Helm Publishers, London, 1979

Goitein, S. D.: *Jews and Arabs: Their Contacts through the Ages.* Schocken Books, New York, 1974

Goreny, Yosef:

- *Zionism and the Arabs, 1882-1948. A Study in Ideology.* Clarendon Press, Oxford, 1987
- *The Arab Question and the Jewish Problem.* Am Oved Publishers, Tel Aviv, 1985

Grossman, David: *Present Absentees.* Ha'kibbutz Ha'meuhad Publishers, Israel, 1992

Hanieh, Akram: "The Camp David Papers." Journal of Palestine Studies 30, Nr. 2, 2001

Hadawi, Sami: *Bitter Harvest, a Modern History of Palestine.* First published in New World Press, 1967. Fifth edition, 1989.

Harkabi J.: *The Palestinian Convention and its Significance.* Israeli Education Ministry Publishers, Jerusalem, 1974

Hassan, N.: Letters from Gaza: An Arsenal of Believers. Talking to the "Human Bombs." In: The New Yorker, November 19, 2004

Heikal, Muhammad Hasnin:

- *The Road to Ramadan.* Collins Publishers, London, 1975
- *The Sphinx and the Commissar: The Rise and Fall of the Soviet Influence in the Arab World.* Am Oved Publishers, Tel Aviv, 1981

Herzl, Theodor:

- *Complete Diaries.* Herzl Press and T. Yoseloff, New York, 1960
- *Diaries, a-c.* Biyalik Institute / The Zionist Library, Jerusalem, 1997

Hourani, Albert: *Arabic Thought in the Liberal Age, 1798-1939.* London, 1962

Horovitz, J.: *The Qur'anic Paradise.* Jerusalem, 1923

Hugi, Jacky: *Arabian Nights.com. The Arab World Today.* Ma'ariv Book guild, Tel Aviv, 2011

Jabotinsky, Zeev: *Documents: on the Way to a State.* Ari Jabotinsky, Jerusalem, 1959

Karmi, H. S.: How Holy is Palestine to the Muslims? Islamic Quarterly

Kassir, S.: *Being Arab.* London/New York, 2006

Kedourie, Elie:

- *England and the Middle East: the Destruction of the Ottoman Empire, 1914-1921.* London, 1956
- *The Arab-Israeli Conflict in Arabic Political Memories.* London, 1974

Kedourie, Fred: *The Arab-Israeli Dilemma.* New York, 1968

Kerr, Malcolm H.: *The Arab Cold War 1958-1967.* 2nd ed., Oxford University Press, New York, 1967

Khalidi, Rashid: *Palestinian Identity.* Columbia U.P., New York, 1997

Khalidi, Walid: Thinking the Unthinkable: A Sovereign Palestinian State. Foreign Affairs 56, 4, July 1978

Kimche, David: *The Last Option: the Fight for Peace in the Middle East.* Yediot Aharonot Publishers, Tel Aviv, 1992

Kimche, Jon and David: *A Clash of Destinies: The Arab-Jewish War and the Foundation of the State of Israel.* Praeger Publishers, New York, 1960

Kraemer, Gudrun:

- *Geschichte Palästinas: History of Palestine.* C. H. Beck Verlag, Munich 2002
- *Demokratie im Islam. Der Kampf für Toleranz und Freuheit in der arabischen Welt.* Verlag C.H.Beck, 2011

Kupferschmidt, Uri M.: *The Supreme Muslim Council: Islam under the British Mandate for Palestine.* E. J. Brill Publishers, Leiden, New York, 1987

Laqueur, Walter: *The Road to Jerusalem.* Macmillan Publishers, 1968

Laroui, Abdullah: *The Crisis of the Arab Intellectual.* Berkeley, University of California Press, 1976

Lewis, Bernard:

- Palestine – History and Geography of a Name. in: "Alei historia" a collection of essays, published by the Yitzhak Ben Zvi Center, Jerusalem, 1988
- *The Emergence of Modern Turkey*. London, 1961

Lohlker, Ruediger:

- *Islam. Eine Ideengeschichte*. Facultas Publisher, Vienna, 2008
- *Islam im Internet. Neue Religionen im Cyberspace*. Hamburg, 2001

Makovsky, David: *Making Peace with the PLO: The Rabin Government's Road to the Oslo Accord.* West View Press, Boulder, Colo. 1996

Mansfield, Peter: *A History of the Middle East*. Penguin Group USA, 2003

Milstein, Uri: *History of the War of Independence*. Vol. 4. University Press of America, 1996-1998

Mishal, Saul: *East Bank West Bank: The Palestinians in Jordan 1949-1967.* Yale University Press, New Haven, 1978

Moris Banny:

- *The Birth of the Palestinian Problem 1947-1949*. Am Oved Publishers, Israel, 1991
- *The Border Wars of Israel 1949-1956*. Am Oved Publishers, Israel, 1996
- *Victims: The History of the Zionist-Arab Conflict. 1881-2001*. Am Oved Publishers, Israel, 2003
- *The Birth of the Palestinian Refugee Problem Revisited*. Cambridge U.P., 2004
- *1948. A History of the First Arab-Israeli War*. Am Oved publishers, Tel Aviv, 2010

Mosab, Hassan Yousef: *Son of Hamas*. Modan Publishers, Israel, 2010

Nahem, Ilan: *Mitzrayim/Egypt*. Education Ministry of the state of Israel, Ben-Zvi Institution together with Hebrew University: Jerusalem 2007

Nasser, Jamal A.: *The Resentful Arab* (Previous title: *The Embittered Arab*), *The Truth about the Palestine Question*. Dar el-Nahar Publishers, Lebanon. Jerusalem-Jordan, 1964

Netanyahu, Benjamin: *A Place under the Sun*. Tel Aviv, 1995

Pail, Meir: "The Israeli Wars – the Yom-Kippur-War." In: *Personalities and Deeds in Israel: Jubilee Book*. By Aharoni Meir and Sara. Miksam Publishers, Israel, 1988

Pedahzur, Reuven: *Victory of Embarrassment: Israel and the Territories after the Six-Day War*. Bitan Publishers, Tel Aviv, 1996

Peretz, Don: *Israel and the Palestine Arabs*. Washington D.C., 1958

Porath, Yehoshua: *The Palestinian Arab National Movement: from Riots to Rebellion, 1929-1939*. Frank Cass Publishers, London 1977

Rabinovich, Itamar:

- *The Road not Taken*. Oxford University Press, Oxford and New York, 1991
- *Waging Peace. (Peace and Normalization), Israel and the Arabs 1948-2003*. Kineret-Zmora-Bitan Publishers, Tel Aviv, 2004
- *Ha'ofek ha'mitrahek: The Lingering Conflict. Israel, the Arabs and the Middle East, 1948-2011*. Kineret, Zmora-Bitan, Dvir Publishers, Tel Aviv 2012

Rodinson, Maxime: *Israel: A Colonial-Settler State?* Monad Press, New York, 1973

Said, Edward:

- *The Question of Palestine*. Routledge & Kegan Paul Publishers, London and Henley, 1880
- *Peace and its Discontents*. Vintage Books, New York, 1995
- *Orientalism*. Vintage Books, New York, 1979
- *The Politics of Dispossession*. New York, 1995

Sakhanini, Halil: *I'm Like This, Gentlemen!* Keter Publishers, Jerusalem, 1990

Sand Shlomo: *When and How the Land of Israel was Invented*? Kinneret, Zmora-Bitan, Dvir Publisher, Israel 2012

Savir, Uri: *Kodem Shalom: Peace First*. Yediot Aharonot Publisher, Tel Aviv 2007

Sayyid, Muhammad Ahmed (Sid): *After the Guns Fall Silent*. Am Oved Publishers, 1976

Sayyid, B. S.: *A Fundamental Fear. Eurocentrism and the Emergence of Islamism*. London, 2003

Scharfstein, Sol: *Chronicle of Jewish History: from the Patriarchs to the 21st Century*. KTAV Publishing hpis, 1997

Shamir, Shimon:

- Article for a symposium of Shilo'ah Institute, Tel Aviv, March 1981
- *A Modern History of the Arabs in the Middle* East. Modan Publishers, Ben-Shemen, Israel, 5725 (1965)

Segev, Tom:

- *1949: The First Israelis*. Domino Publishers, Jerusalem, 1984
- *1967 – and the Country Changed Its Face*. Keter Publishers, Israel, 2005

Shiff, Zeev and Yaari, Ehud: *Intifada*. Shoken Publishers, Tel Aviv, 1990

Shlaim, Avi:

- *The Iron Wall*. Miscal Publishers, Tel Aviv, 2000
- *Collision across the Jordan*. Columbia University Press, New York, 1988

Shepherd, Naomi: *Ploughing Sand: British Rule in Palestine, 1917-1948*. New Brunswick, N.J., Rutgers University Press, 2000

Smith, Charles D.: *Palestine and the Arab-Israeli Conflict*. (Sixth Edition) Bedford/St. Martin's publishers, Boston, New York, 2007

Steinberg, Matti: *Facing their Fate. Palestinian National Consciousness 1967-2007*. Yediot Aharonot Publishers, Tel Aviv, 2008

Stendhell, Zeev: *The Founding Myths of Israel: Nationalism, Socialism and the Making of a Jewish State*. Princeton, 1998

Temperley, H.: *England and the Near East*, Vol. I., London, 1936

Stevens, Richard P.: *American Zionism and U.S. Foreign Policy 1942-1947*. New York, 1962

Vassiliev, Alexei: *Russian Police in the Middle East: From Messianism to Pragmatism*. Ithaka Press, 1993

Weizmann, Chaim:

- *Trial and Error: The Autobiography of Chaim Weizmann*. Harper and Brothers, New York, 1949

- *Skies and Earth for You*. Maariv Publishers, Tel Aviv, 1975
- *The Fight for Peace*. Idanim Publishers, Jerusalem, 1981

Yehoshua, A. B.: *Between Right and Right*. Schocken Publishers, Tel Aviv, 1980

Zayyad, Tawfiq: Fate of the Arabs in Israel. Journal of Palestine Studies, VI, I, autumn 1976

The Sunday Times London, June 19, 1977

Other References

Books:

The Bible

The Qur'an

Encyclopedia of Islam

Encyclopedia Judaica

History of the Jewish People. Edited by: H. Ben-Sasson. Three volumes. Dvir Publishers, Tel Aviv, 1969

Dictionaries

Web sites

Newspapers / Magazines:

Haaretz

Journal of Palestine Studies. Published jointly by the Institute of Palestine Studies and Kuwait University.

The Jerusalem Quarterly by Sayigh Yazid, London 1977

PLO Research Center, Sha'on Palestina, Nr. 1-243, Beirut, Nicosia, 1971-1993

Films:

The Gate Keepers, Dror Moreh (director), Israel, 2013

Jews & Muslims, Emanuel Blanchare (director), Arte, 2013.

Arabische Welt - Arab World

ISSN 2199-4013

Band 1

1	Alisa Douer	Ägypten - die verlorene Heimat. Der Exodus aus Ägypten, 1947-1967 ISBN 978-3-8325-3731-9	43.00 EUR
2	Alisa Douer	Egypt - The Lost Homeland: Exodus from Egypt, 1947-1967. The History of the Jews in Egypt, 1540 BCE to 1967 CE ISBN 978-3-8325-4052-4	40.50 EUR